TAKING CONTROL

We feel in colour!

We don't live with BPD... BPD lives with us.

When Is enough, enough?

WHEN YOU SAY IT IS!

I would like to take this opportunity to thank you for purchasing this book and in doing so supporting and raising awareness of Borderline Personality Disorder/Emotionally Unstable Personality Disorder.

I believe that BPD is nothing to fear, instead to be embraced!

Taking Back Control- BPD

Uniquely written with love!

By Emma Warren

Taking back control

For BPD/EUPD

Dedication

I would like to dedicate this book to

Borderline Arts

I have been service user of Borderline Arts.

I'm very thankful for the support I have received through the charity.

Through Borderline Arts I have had the opportunity to be heard and feel noticed. I have had access to creative outlets. I have been able to meet others with BPD and felt less alone but most of all I have found a welcoming and friendly place where I can just be myself. <3

Copyrights

Copyright © 2020 Emma Warren

All rights reserved. No part of this publication may be reproduced, distributed, or transmitted in any form or by any means, including photocopying, recording, or other electronic or mechanical methods, without the prior written permission of the publisher, except in the case of brief quotations embodied in critical reviews and certain other noncommercial uses permitted by copyright law.

Published in the UK

ISBN: 9798655186736

Disclaimers

The publishers and authors are providing this book and its contents on an "as is" basis and make no representations or guarantees of any kind with respect to this book or its contents. The publishers and authors disclaim all such representations and guarantees, including but not limited to guarantees of healthcare for a particular purpose. In addition, the publishers and authors assume no responsibility for errors, inaccuracies, omissions, or any other inconsistencies herein.

The content of this book is for informational purposes only and is not intended to diagnose, treat, cure, or prevent any condition or mental illness. You understand that this book is not intended as a substitute for consultation with a licensed practitioner. Please consult with a healthcare professional regarding the suggestions and recommendations made in this book. The use of this book implies your acceptance of this disclaimer.

The publishers and authors make no guarantees concerning the level of success you may experience by following the advice and strategies contained in this book, and you accept the risk that results will differ for each individual. The testimonials and examples provided in this book show exceptional results, which may not apply to the average reader, and are not intended to represent or guarantee that you will achieve the same or similar results.

Taking Back Control- BPD

Contents List

Introduction... Page (9)

Chapter 1: Umbrella of Self-care... Page (19)

Chapter 2: Self-talk & coping techniques for generalised mental health... Page (39)

Chapter 3: Creative Expressive Arts... Page (65)

Chapter 4: Self-doubt VS Self-belief... Page (81)

Chapter 5: Recognising and managing BPD emotions

Part 1... Page (107)

Part 2... Page (130)

Chapter 6: Taking back control and making something beautiful with BPD Page... (175)

Love for ASD... Page (199)

Taking Back Control- BPD

Taking Back Control- BPD

Introduction

Taking Back Control- BPD

About the author

Emma Warren

I want to take the time to thank you for reading this book, I have come so very far on my journey of self-discovery and I want to help you to do the same. My name is Emma, I'm 28 and I live in the UK. I'm a single mother to my beautiful little boy. I am currently studying for my Psychology with Counselling Honours degree. Are you asking yourself why should I take advice from a young student? Believe me, I have asked myself this question on your behalf many times! My only answer is that I have come from a place of pain. I have asked the same questions you are asking yourself and I have sought to answer them. It is only through doing so that I have learned and practiced new things and made many lifestyle changes. I believe in this advice I am passing on to you for one simple reason... It has changed my life.

Pictured here is my son Finley, our dog Bear and I.

My vision & reason for writing this book

I am so passionate about people having access to support due to my own not-so-good experiences of mental health support. I realise that I am only one individual and I alone cannot change the way a society runs its mental health services, but my mission is to simply offer hope and encourage people to help themselves. Ultimately, mental health support these days is very few and far between and people are not getting the support they need. So many people want to be 'better', but they simply do not know how. It is my vision to help people. Not in the sense a therapist would but to provide practical support and coping strategies for people with Borderline Personality Disorder. I have also included a love for Autism Spectrum Disorder section because ASD has become such a huge part of my personal life and carries such an important place in my journey of life to date. I want to share my knowledge in the hope that it will reassure you, comfort you and inspire you.

I am not a psychologist; I am not a therapist and I am not a teacher. I am one individual that has a Borderline Personality Disorder diagnosis, and I am a mother to my son who has an Autism Spectrum Disorder diagnosis. I am an overcomer of fear, I am a believer in hope, and I am a survivor through pain. I have battled anxiety; I have been underestimated more times than I can count but I have prevailed. I have a voice and I am here to use it to help people who want it.

I have drawn from my own experiences; I have inspired change in my own live, and I am going to share this with you. My book is for anyone and everyone because we can all hit a brick wall at some point of our lives. Although I welcome everybody to read this book, I must state that the book is aimed at supporting Borderline Personality Disorder with a touch of love for ASD. If you have an explosion of emotions that leave you feeling out of control, low self-esteem, zero confidence and you have ever felt like you are not enough for this world, then this is the book for you. In this book I will provide you with the tools that'll aim to help you overcome these struggles and I will explain step by step how to use them. All you have to do is keep an open mind, open yourself up to the possibility of change and find the courage to practice.

You can totally change your life and take back control, believe me you can…
I wish you luck and hope you find the learnings within this book successful.

Borderline Arts

I'm Sarah and I founded the charity 'Borderline Arts'. I had experienced first-hand a great deal of stigma due to my mental health difficulties and having BPD in particular. In early 2013 Artcore UK got in touch with me and asked me to exhibit some of my artwork to help viewers gain an understanding of different peoples' mental health issues. I was hit by how powerfully this raised the public's awareness of mental health difficulties and therefore reduced associated stigma.

I got friends involved, and we held another exhibition and began to run workshops and a theatre group and 'Borderline Arts' quickly became more established.

Taking Back Control- BPD

Our aim always being to use the arts to reduce stigma surrounding Borderline Personality Disorder (BPD). We later moved into an office premises and became a registered charity!

Over seven years later, we continue to run various events and activities. We still run occasional exhibitions of art created by those with BPD. The purpose of this is to enable some really talented artists to express their first-hand experience of BPD in a media that, for some, says much more than words can, and as I mentioned before, raises the public's awareness of BPD and therefore reduces the associated stigma.

We run regular creative groups for those diagnosed with the condition. These groups are not therapy groups to explore difficulties, but rather a space to focus on positive elements of ourselves and our lives. We create art to explore/express our qualities, interests, quirks, happy memories, healthy relationships etc. We have chosen this focus, as many of us with BPD struggle to know who we are outside of the BPD label. Much of the time we can even feel that we are 'innately bad'. We want to strengthen the realisation that the diagnosis of BPD is essentially a list of (often overwhelming) difficulties we are faced with, but that it does not define who we are!

We also run creative educational workshops for professionals working with individuals with BPD. These workshops combine giving theoretical information about the conditions with creative activities and many first-hand experiences shared by facilitators who live with BPD on a daily basis. This enables participants to gain a much greater and deeper understanding of the condition and to develop improved relationships with those they are supporting and offer much more effective help and treatment as a result.

Another of the strands of Borderline Arts is 'Theatre'. Through our theatre performances, as is the case in all we do, we aim to raise awareness of and break down stigma surrounding Borderline Personality Disorder. Our current project is a short film based around a Dialectical Behaviour Therapy Group, in which all the participants have BPD. It explores the different sides of the condition through a film and some real-life interviews. We see the main characters' experiences and stories and their journey through the health system. Our aim with this piece is to raise awareness and get people talking and asking questions about BPD, perhaps also challenging the current healthcare system, and ultimately showing that people with BPD are just people!

Setting up and running Borderline Arts has been a journey and there have been great highs and lows - running a charity is not easy, and when you add in living with a diagnosis of BPD, it certainly adds another dimension of challenges! But with an amazing team of volunteers, Borderline Arts is thriving.

Taking Back Control- BPD

Taking Back Control- BPD

Chapter 1: Umbrella of Self-care

"Authenticity is the daily practice of letting go of who we think we're supposed to be and embracing who we are." Brené Brown

Taking Back Control- BPD

Authentic Self

Your authentic self means being true to yourself despite other people's expectations of you. It can be so easy these days to try and make yourself fit into a society which has predetermined social norms and structured rules. This is almost what we are expected to do, however, as we know, having BPD is not always allowing of us to conform within these expectations. Having said this, I believe that having BPD is not a limitation, it's a strength. Having the ability to experience extreme emotions means we are able to love more, hope more and flourish through our strong determination. If we channel the best parts of our emotions within ourselves, we can experience, without fear, that we can "fit" into this society through being our authentic selves.

Being your authentic self doesn't mean that we solely have to adhere to this society, it's about being ourselves in society and not what society wants us to be. It's also important to remain true to yourself, even in your own company, when the outside world doesn't matter, you do you... because you do you best. You are entitled and deserving, and it is your birthright to be who YOU want to be.

Your authentic self comes from being aware and self-acceptance. As we accept our best qualities, we must also accept our worse. It's not about striving for perfection it's about accepting our uniqueness as a whole and learning to thrive with all our abilities in check. Ultimately, we can choose who we want to be, and we don't have to be defined by other people. We can be our best selves even when we are not when we learn that sometimes we are not okay, and we are accepting of this. If we embrace all of who we are, accept and love ourselves, then we become our authentic selves.

What is self-care?

Let's get down to basics!

Basic self-care is a necessary requirement to be able to function to the best of our abilities. It's vital that we allow ourselves the time to rest, reflect and revitalise. Our bodies are like are homes and are therefore sacred. We must protect, love and care for our bodies. This means getting ample amount of sleep, following good sleeping patterns and making sure you have a healthy balanced diet. We should include time to exercise daily, this has been proven to release chemicals such as dopamine and endorphins and improve mental state.

Nurturing our bodies is just as important as nurturing our minds. Equally, our minds need space, calmness and time to process and reflect in order for them to also be working to the best of their abilities. Finding time to self-care is important but is also very enjoyable.

So, what is self-care?

Self-care is about allowing yourself the time to do something for you. As mentioned previously, it can be effective for self-reflection and giving yourself some space. It can also be allowing yourself the time to do something you enjoy. These can be things such as, creative arts, exercise and sports, having a bath, reading, gardening and so on. In essence, it is anything you enjoy, that makes you feel good and helps you feel like you again.

Personally, I enjoy singing. This is something that always lifts my mood, brings me back to being me and I find it very freeing. Sometimes a combination of self-care activities, such as, singing to Disney in the bath whilst watching as your favorite coloured bath bomb disperses into the water can increase the levels of self-care and in doing so creating more of an all-round self-care experience. I feel that this can take you to another headspace where you are engaging all your senses, being present in the moment and making the most of your self-care time.

Why is self-care so important?

Self-care is important for everyone's mental wellbeing, but I feel like it is more so when it comes to having BPD. I believe this because we must allow ourselves the emotional outlet in a safe space where we can then continue to maintain our positive emotional stability. Self-caring is a non-judgmental, personal and essential experience of our own which we must allow time for.

Self-care forms the basis of our physical and mental wellbeing and is at the very heart of the process towards taking back control.

Self-love

Self-love is an important part of Self-care, although they are two completely different things, they both cannot be fully integrated into your all-round wellbeing without one another. Self-love is something people say they cannot fully understand or are able to do entirely. It's true that self-love takes a lot of practice and determination. You have to find it within yourself, which can be especially hard if you don't feel you have any self-worth. Self-love requires you to find a respect for yourself and to show unconditional love to yourself.

The question to start by asking yourself is... do you love others? like your family, unconditionally?

Presumably, the answer to this question is YES

Now ask yourself...do you love yourself? unconditionally?

It's a much harder question to answer isn't it? Why is it easier to love others than yourself? Mostly it comes down to the fact that we don't see ourselves like we see others. We aren't always as positive as we should be, and we miss the points about us that make us worthy and valuable people. The thing to remember is that we are all equals in this world. It doesn't matter who has the better house, more money, the seemingly perfect marriage, the power job roles within society or how educated a person is. Honestly, these things are not important. When it comes to things and money, we are born into this world with nothing and we leave this world with nothing. Love is the only thing we are born with and the only thing we die with. A newborn infant instinctively attaches to its caregiver and not just because they provide the basic essentials like food. There is a study conducted using monkey's, in which the experimenter placed two robot mothers into the habitat of infant monkeys. One mother provided the food but was made from wired metal that the monkeys could cling to and drink milk from the bottle. The other mother didn't have any food attached, however, was made out of soft terry cloth where the infant monkeys would feel comforted from this. When the wired mother along with the food were removed from the habitat the infants didn't seem bothered. When the terry cloth mother was removed from the habitat instead, the infants would cry and become very distressed. The study is interesting because it's shows us that infants do not just attach to their caregivers because they provide the basic essentials, but they form attachments through comfort and love first and foremost. We as humans are designed to survive through love and we cannot live without it. One of the reasons we aim to get a nice house, a decent job, an education and such is to provide for our families and to enjoy our own lives with our families. So, you can see how love takes the seemingly important aspects out of life like money. The wealthiest man on the planet couldn't survive alone without love.

So, what does the above have to do with self-love?

When we love ourselves, we can be more loving towards others and in turn others are more loving towards us. Money doesn't make the world go round; love does!

We seem to struggle with the idea of self-love because isn't putting yourself first selfish?

The truth is if we don't put ourselves first, then we are not able to self-love or self-care for ourselves and then we are not able to love or care for others. For instance, in the event of a plane crash it's said that you need to fit your own oxygen mask before fitting your child's. It goes against all parents' initial thoughts where they would do something for their child first before themselves. It is a crucial point to make here because actually putting yourself first is more important. As the plane crash example demonstrates, if you aren't able to breathe then you aren't able to help your child to either. Learning to self-love ourselves is learning to put ourselves first so we can then give to others.

Self-love is the way you feel about yourself. Unconditionally loving yourself is easier said than done. We tend to find it easier to hate ourselves for our flaws and mistakes. If you're a parent or have children who you are close to, we may find ourselves angry or disappointed if they have done something wrong, but we do not love them any less because of it. We forgive them, we help them to understand that what they've done is wrong so they can learn from it. Through this, the child looks to you for guidance, support and encouragement. This is unconditional love, our love only grows for them, their wrong doings do not make us love them any less. We must use this as a platform to help us with our own unconditional self-love, we must forgive ourselves for our mistakes, accept our flaws and give ourselves guidance and encouragement instead of tearing ourselves down. Self-love is the way we feel about ourselves; self-care is the way we treat ourselves; they are different things, but they need each other. They both work hand in hand and you deserve self-care and self-love, you have infinite worth and you are loved.

Taking Back Control- BPD

I'm learning to love myself

Written By Emma Warren
(Post-diagnosis, aged 27, February 2020)

I'm learning to love myself,
It's an ongoing process that doesn't end,
It's one of the hardest things to do,
I have many barriers to break through.

I'm learning to love myself,
I choose my clothing with care,
I take pride in my appearance,
Maintaining takes a little perseverance.

I'm learning to love myself,
By finding time for things I enjoy,
Self-care can go a long way,
Especially when I've had a really hard day.

I'm learning to love myself,
I worry about people judging me,
I try self-talk to calm my mind,
Drowning out negativity and being kind.

I'm learning to love myself,
I've always been loving to others,
But it's hard to take my own love,
That I feel I'm undeserving of.

I'm learning to love myself,
By accepting the things I cannot change,
And taking control over the things I can,
I'm patient and a stronger woman.

I'm learning to love myself,
I recognise the hard times I've had,
I am proud I have come through,
I learn from my past, I'm grateful and start anew.

Taking Back Control- BPD

I'm learning to love myself,
It's an ongoing process that doesn't end,
Finding the right balance and taking it slow,
Everyday a little more love will grow.

I'm learning to love myself,
It's one of the hardest things to do,
But I remind myself what I've already come through
And when I look into the mirror now, I say...
I love you

Positive self-image

Self-image is the way we see ourselves. When you look in the mirror do you like what you see? It's so easy to pick faults with yourself isn't it? Self-imagine doesn't just come down to the way we feel about the way we look it's also down how we think of ourselves. Meaning, do we view ourselves as intelligent or stupid? Do we view ourselves as having a positive mentality or a negative one? How do we see ourselves sexually? How do we view our abilities and skills? How do we view our values? Self-image is down to how we see ourselves as a whole. Having BPD can often bring distortion to our self-image and how we feel one day may not be how we feel the next. Identity as a whole can often be confusing to those of us with the condition and we linger on that very difficult question of- Who am I? But just because we experience an unstable self-image doesn't mean that we cannot have a positive self-image. We may change our minds on certain things in a matter of minutes or weeks, but change doesn't have to have negative impact.

A positive self-image requires you to think about what you like about yourself rather than dislike.

Taking Back Control- BPD

Things to take into account:

1. What are your values?

Your values determine how you live your life, so if you value family then you can class yourself a very family orientated person.

2. What are your strengths and positive qualities?

Everyone has strengths and weaknesses. You should identify your strengths and focus on these instead of your weaknesses. Remember weaknesses can turn into positives. Take note of your positive qualities, if you struggle, try asking a friend, our friends sometimes see us in a completely different light from what we see ourselves in.

3. What physical appearances do you like about yourself?

Remember you're unique and don't compare yourself to others.

4. What do you enjoy?

What we enjoy often says a lot about who we are or who we aspire to be. Use your enjoyments to be your authentic self and to inspire your future.

5. What things have you done to improve your life?

Remember how far you've come. Congratulate yourself for your achievements. Be proud that you've made positive improvements in your life.

Acceptance plays a massive part with our distorted self-image. There are going to be days where we don't appreciate ourselves as much. We can either accept these thoughts and keep our self-image stable by knowing that these thoughts will pass. Or we can challenge these thoughts. There isn't a right or wrong and you should do which ever you deem appropriate. We are allowed to change our minds, what we enjoy today may be different to what we enjoy in a couple of months. It's not about WHAT we enjoy, it's about DOING what we enjoy, whatever it may be at the current time. The main point to take away is that shifting self-image is perfectly okay if we try and keep it positive in the process. Having a healthy self-image is accepting flaws, insecurities and focusing on your strengths, positive qualities and attributes and remaining true to your values.

So that famously difficult question of- Who am I?

You already know!

I know who I am

Taking Back Control- BPD

Having a positive self-image can be difficult. The external as well as the internal pressures we come across can arise from self-doubt and expectations of ourselves are sometimes met and other times not. At times we find ourselves living up to our expectations, other times we find that we fall short and occasionally we exceed our expectations. Often experiencing the highs and lows of these points along our journeys is similarly comparable to a game of snakes and ladders. We never know what life is going to throw our way. Sometimes we can find ourselves moving up the ladders or unfortunately sliding down the snakes, however, we keep going. The only way to go is up, we keep going and we do not give in!

Tailored Care Package

Making a tailored care package is a fun way to try and bring a little self-love and care into your life. Being a distraction in themselves in the initial planning and creation stages, it can be a comfort knowing it's there at your disposal. It's possible you may have come across tailored care packages under a different name, maybe a comfort box or an emergency care kit. It's true that there are many names for them, and they all pretty much offer the same sort of thing. However, the beauty of a tailored care package is that you can create this package in line with your own requirements, even down to the fine details of the box decoration as well as it's contents.

I have split some suggestions into sub-categories to inspire you. You may wish use different contents and that's absolutely fine! Firstly, you need to consider what sort of box you wish to use, a big one? A small one? Maybe a bag if you wish to take it places with you, or all the above, there's nothing wrong with having a few for different purposes!

Sensory
- Fidget cubes
- Rubber bands
- Bubble wrap
- Sensory bottles
- Feathers
- Stress ball
- Playdough
- Slime
- Pottery clay

Therapeutic distractions
- Books/audio books
- Poems
- Colouring
- Drawing
- Painting
- Baking kits/recipe cards
- Meditations

Taking Back Control - BPD

- Notebook & pen

Food & Drink (comfort food)
- Chocolate
- Sweets
- Soup
- Hot Choc/favourite tea/coffee
- Your favourite mug
- Cookbook

Entertainment
- Music
- Films
- Puzzles
- Favourite games

Sentimental
- Teddy Bear
- Cards from loved ones
- Letter to self
- Photos
- Sentimental keepsakes

Pampering
- Soft blanket
- Luxury pajamas
- Slippers
- Bath bombs
- Incense
- Face mask
- Manicure & pedicure set
- Soaps/Bath gels

Money
- For things that can't be kept in the box (ice-cream, flowers, cakes etc.)
- To treat yourself (retail therapy!)

I hope you have as much fun as I do with creating your own tailored care packages, they are such a great thing to do for yourself and using them will increase your self-care levels.

The self-care umbrella

In this chapter we have addressed what self-care is. We have looked at things all fitting into the umbrella of self-care. Authentic self, self-love, positive self-image, physical care and mentality care. They all hold an equal segment of umbrella, meaning they all are equally important, and they are all needed to complete the umbrella of self-care.

They all work in sync with one another and we need to remember that we are always changing and growing and through all of this our self-care is at the core of our ability to do so. Self-care forms the basis of our physical and mental wellbeing and is at the very heart of the process towards taking back control. Take your self-care seriously, this should be a priority!

…

Taking Back Control- BPD

Chapter 2: Self-talk & Coping Techniques for generalised mental health

"Whether you think you can or you can't. You're right." Henry Ford

Taking Back Control- BPD

What is self-talk?

Self-talk is simply what it says it is. It's you talking to yourself in your mind. You know that little voice that is continuously non-stop in your head all day, every day. It always seems to get louder when you're trying to have a moment's peace and typically when you are trying to go to sleep. It is constantly nagging at you to do this or do that. It's never shuts up!

Yep that's the one; it has always been with you. It's like your conscience talking out loud to you. It's the voice of power within you that can be so compelling over you. Your self-talk is very persuasive, it can persuade you to right but equally it can persuade you to wrong. It's reasonable VS un-reasonable, logical VS illogical and judgmental VS open-minded.

It can be many things but what I would like you to focus on is positive talk VS negative talk when it comes to yourself. How do you use your self-talk? Are you kind to yourself? Or can you be quite hard on yourself? The way we self-talk to ourselves is very important. In a way it's like the voice of our inner child. Some may be strict with their inner child whilst others may be softer.

Taking Back Control- BPD

Inner child visualisation exercise

You may wish to firstly record yourself saying the visualisation so that you can listen back with your eyes closed.

I want you to close your eyes and picture yourself as a child, the child is standing in front of you, you as you are now are standing about a meter away. The child isn't making eye contact with you and keeps looking down towards the floor. I want you to now talk to the child as if you would self-talk to yourself when you are being strict. Try to capture the same tone and the same words you may use whatever they may be.
Now notice how this makes you feel. Do you feel guilty for having spoken to the child in that way? Did it bring a feeling of upsetting uncomfortableness? Really take the time here to notice how you are feeling, I realise this is not easy and personally when I tried this it was quite discomforting.
You see the child in front of you start to cry, this troubles you and you try to offer comfort by apologising. The child looks up at you making direct eye contact this time with their tears falling slowly down. They start to say something 'I... I... I...' but they cannot speak what they are trying to say. You take a step forward and crouch down to their level and make direct eye contact right back. You gently ask the child to try to talk again. The child's tears begin to come to a stop and as they reach out their hands to hold yours. They attempt to speak again, this time saying, 'I forgive you'. You breathe a sigh of relief as you hear the words. Again, just like before, take a moment here to suss out how you are feeling.
You take a moment to think and then you respond to the child by saying 'you're okay now'. The child smiles up at you before reaching their arms around you and hugging you. As this is a younger version of yourself you feel very connected. You are surprised by the love you feel for the child knowing that it is yourself and you almost feel like you want to protect the child. You wish you can tell the child what is to come in the hope that they can change this. You feel sorry for the child that they have still so much yet to come. However, you realise that this is just not possible, and you cannot change what has already occurred.
You are still hugging the child and you stand up whilst cradling the child in your arms as if they were your own child. The child is comforted by this. The child picks their head up so to look at you whilst they are still in your arms. Looking at you with an expression of confusion they ask, 'Are we okay?' You smile at the child before you place them back on their feet. As they stand in front of you once more you respond, 'We are okay, we have always been okay, and we will always be okay'. The child gives you the biggest smile reaching from cheek to cheek, their eyes now dry and beaming with a hopeful glow. Then they turn around and walk away from you. As they walk into the distance they fade away and you watch as they disappear as if they were never even there with you.
Notice once more how you are feeling from this. Just feel what you feel in this moment and try to process this. Now repeatedly say to yourself out loud or in your head 'I am okay' until you start to feel some comfort from this.

Did you understand the purpose of this exercise?

The point of this exercise is for you to try and get in touch with the negative self-talk that comes from within you. It's to give you the chance to realise that when you self-talk in this negative way that you are creating a message that is un-reassuring. It is a visualisation tool to support you in the process of learning to forgive yourself for your previous harsh self-talk. You are that child; you are that forgiving child, and you are that child that needed reassurance that you are okay. Essentially, it was you forgiving yourself for your discouraging and unfriendly self-talk that you have used unnecessarily.

Imagine yourself as the child when you use negative self-talk because as a child is innocently impressionable, frightened and confused, so are you even if you don't realise it. Everything you have learned from when you were a small child has influenced the way you think and the way you talk to yourself. Maybe you learned from your parents that you need to be strict on yourself to achieve something. Maybe you have self-created this from your own fears of being not good enough. You've put yourself under pressure to perform to a certain standard and now you have incorporated it into your way of thinking. Maybe it has come from past mistakes, previous wrong judgments or not so good experiences and you are trying not to repeat these. You have developed this way of self-talking over many years and it's understandable that you are sometimes a little too hard on yourself, after all we want to be the best that can be, don't we? So why is it wrong?

Negative self-talk can be consuming in a way that will always keep you stuck in a place where you feel like you're not good enough and that you can't do anything. It doesn't matter whether we are using the negative self-talk to try and be better or prevent something from going wrong. Sure, if it works, you find that it can sometimes be helpful, but chances are it is not going to work all the time. Believe it or not we tend to perform worse when we put this pressure on ourselves. So, what happens on the times this strict mentality doesn't come through for you? Do you result in coming down even harder on yourself than previously? If you continued to do this, you would continue to get harder and harder and harder on yourself until there would be nothing, but utter resentment left for yourself. You will always be stuck in a place where you will never be good enough because you will never be good enough for yourself.

We need to be forgiving of ourselves when something has gone wrong or is going wrong. We need to reassure ourselves that we are okay because this is comforting. Just like the child, we need comfort. We need to love ourselves just like the child needed love. We all have an inner child and although we want to protect the child, we equally want to encourage the child so they can learn to be independent. We need to be nurturing, offer a soft kindness, show understanding and provide encouraging reassurance.

Did you notice in the visualisation how the words for the speech changed as you went through? At first you said to the child 'You're okay now', followed by 'We are okay, we have always been okay, and we will always be okay' and lastly 'I am okay'.

The benefits of positive self-talk

Positive self-talk can benefit us in a number of ways. Not only can it improve our mental state and enhance our optimistic mentality, but it can help with general wellbeing also. Self-talk is something we have developed over a lifetime and so negative self-talk can be hard to break. However, with this being said, just as you learned negative self-talk over a number of years, positive self-talk can also be learned. Positive self-talk can be formed from gaining perspective of the situation. You have to consciously make the effort to change the way you internally talk to yourself. At first your thoughts will always follow the same pattern of thinking you have been used to and this is okay. Allow the thoughts to enter your mind and recognise that they are present.

Taking Back Control- BPD

Let's take a moment to look at what is meant by negative self-talk:

- Labelling- This means to label yourself as something that is negative.
  Examples: I'm stupid, I'm ugly, I'm a horrible person, etc.
- Blaming- Blaming yourself for things that go wrong or if you make a mistake.
  Examples: It's all my fault, why did I do that for?!, I've really messed up this time, etc.
- Negative/fearful association - This is down to a past experience where it didn't quite go to plan and so when the same or similar situation arises you have a negative association to it.
  Examples: I can't go to the dentist because last time it hurt me, I can't put in for my driving test again because I keep failing, I don't like to play football anymore because I broke my leg playing when I was child, etc.
- Magnifying- When magnifying the situation, we tend to view the situation as worse than it actually is.
  Example: I've run out of money and I don't get paid for another three days, what am I going to do?
- Catastrophising- Similar to magnification but on a higher level. It's usually a series of thoughts that go downhill from the original thought.
  Example: I can't get the car to start, I'm going to be late for work, I'm going to lose my job, I'll not be able to pay to get the car repaired, I'll not be able to pay for anything, I'll fall in debt, I'll end up losing everything….
- Punishment- What is meant by punishment is the continuous feed of negative thoughts that repeatedly beat you down about something once experienced over and over again.
  Example: This one is a difficult one to

example because it can be anything unhelpful that you play on a loop to yourself. I'm going to use a personal example of one of my own. When I was 14, a teacher of mine noticed that I felt awkward at the start of a class. She came up to me in the school hall where the class was taking place and said, 'If you don't know what to do then get a chair and sit in the middle of the hall.' So, I got a chair and sat in the middle of the hall where my class peers all stood around the outside of the hall looking in. I felt singled out, made Centre of attention and thoughts that everyone was laughing at me creeped in. I actually ended up walking out and for years after this is what would play in my mind whenever I would feel awkward in public. I'd have this teacher's voice playing in my mind saying again 'If you don't know what to do then get a chair and sit in the middle' however over time It had turned into a punishment to myself for not knowing how to function in public. The statement changed over time to 'go sit in the middle so everyone can laugh at you for not knowing what to do'

- Self-doubting- self-doubt can be present when you don't even realise it and self-doubt can present itself through self-talk and keep us stuck in that negative mentality.
Examples: I can't do it, I'm not good enough, I'm worthless, they will always be better than me, etc.
- Negative emotional response- This can be any sort of negative response however during times of frustration or anger the negative self-talk can be more noticeable.
Examples: I'm so angry, I'm really annoyed, I feel disappointed, I'm so depressed, I can't believe this is happening, I can't get over it, etc.

As you can see from the examples there are many occasions where negative self-talk can be present. You may almost feel bombarded from the list of the range of negative self-talk reasons. However just be assured that for every negative there is a positive alternative. Try to be open-minded and optimistic with this. Now we aren't going to rid our thought process of these thoughts entirely however we can choose to be more sympathetic about what we are thinking and how we are feeling. Following this we can shift our thoughts to try and see the situation from a different perspective. We can offer ourselves an alternative thought that is going to provide us with reassurance instead of fueling our negativity. If you already feel bad about a situation then why would you want to make yourself feel worse? We are not helping ourselves by lingering on this sort of thinking. To change these thoughts around we do not have to disregard how we feel about the situation. We can become aware of how we feel, recognise the feelings that are coming up with these thoughts and learn to accept them. Control how you internalise these feelings. Sympathise with yourself, show understanding, provide comfort and forgive yourself. It is okay that this negative self-talk is present right now. It is part of the process of becoming aware, once aware this gives you the chance to change your thoughts to kinder alternative thoughts.

Taking Back Control- BPD

Let's take a look at some positive self-talk we can use as an alternative against the previous examples:

Negative Self-talk	Positive Self-talk
Labelling- I'm stupid	I'm learning
Blaming- I really messed up this time	I let this go. I forgive myself and learn from my mistakes.
Negative/fearful association	I will rewrite my negative associations with positive associations. I can change it.
Magnifying- I don't get paid until another three days, what am I going to do?	I am resourceful. I find opportunity in the challenges presented to me.
Catastrophising	I'm going to stop for a moment and breathe. I will remain calm and focus my mind to finding a solution. I can do this.
Punishment	I will let go of unhelpful thoughts. I can get through this now. I am safe now. I trust in myself to create new positive experiences in the present.
Self-doubt- I'm worthless	I am as equal as anyone else in this world. I am loved and I have worth.
Negative emotional response	I'm taking a moment to bring calm and quiet to myself. I know that by remaining calm I can stay in control. I am taking back control.

Self-talk is powerful. It can impact you both negatively and positively. What do you choose to give power to? Accept that your negative self-talk is there and forgive yourself for these thoughts. Let go of these thoughts and then bring in power to positive alternatives. The use of positive self-talk takes daily practice and patience. You are trying to retrain your pattern of thinking of many years. Trust that it will get easier the more you practice. Trust that it will improve your mentality and provide reassurance and comfort in your times of need. Trust that you are able to gain perspective, that you can remain calm and take back control. Trust in positive self-talk, give power to it and use it to help you move forward.

Coping Techniques
(Physical symptoms)

"When life decides to be harder... decide yourself to be stronger." Emma Warren

Breathing- Inhale for 4 seconds, hold for 2 and exhale for 4 seconds. If you find the amount of seconds challenging due to physical health or any other reason, then please change these timings to something more suitable. The key here is to take deep breaths and to slow the breathing down. This will help you feel calmer and more in control. It has been helpful to me to imagine colours as I breathe. On the inhale I imagine breathing in cool, calming blue. On the exhale I imagine breathing out red. I associate the red to whatever I'm feeling at the time, anger, jealousy, anxiety or any other negative emotion.

Bracelets/fidget objects- I often find my hands become sweaty and I aimlessly wonder what to do with them. I wear bracelets on my wrist and find that playing with these is helpful. It keeps my hands busy while my minds trying to process what I'm thinking. I know that fidget cubes are very popular so you could also use these. The problem I found with fidget cubes was that they created unwanted attention. People would often ask me why I was playing with the cube or why I thought I needed one. It can be an obvious sign that you feel uncomfortable which personally I would rather people remain unaware of.

Walk it out- walk it out while you work it out. Your body may start to shake, or your muscles may become tense or you may experience twitching. You may find your body becomes quite frantic and you are unsure what you should do with your body. Try going for a short walk. Do this to give yourself time to process so your body is doing one thing whilst allowing chance for your mind to do the other. It may also interest you to know that walking releases endorphins into the body and improves mood. It is also proven that walking increases serotonin levels in the brain which also influence mood.

Practice star jumping- I realise that this sounds like a bit of an odd exercise to consider doing but honestly it can help. If you are in a situation where there are others you may wish to take yourself elsewhere to do this one. I am not ashamed to say that I have once done my star jumping in the cubicle of a ladies public toilet! The idea around the star jumping is it forces your body into thinking it needs to focus on doing the exercises you are giving it and, in the process, forgets about the other things that are going on. The body essentially puts effort into trying to take deep breaths while you are exercising it. Also, on an additional note you can find humour in however ridiculous you feel doing your star jumps to help lighten your mood.

Ground yourself- Grounding yourself means to bring yourself back to reality. Have you ever walked into a supermarket and found that the lighting can be really disorientating and suddenly you feel like your surroundings are like a dream like state? I have had this many times and I find certain lighting can be a trigger along with crowded public spaces. You can use grounding techniques whenever you feel like this and it will help alleviate some anxiety. To ground myself I usually work through my senses and connect them to something around me. What can you see? Notice something, even if it's small, focus on this and allow yourself to take it in. Look at all the colours for a moment, and then move on. What can you hear? Choose to drown out all exterior noises and try focusing on one and then maybe a couple. What can you smell? What can you feel? And so on. This sounds quite lengthy in my description, but it doesn't have to be, and you don't have to necessarily stop what you're doing to do them. Find a way to incorporate them into whatever you're doing.

Coping techniques for intrusive thoughts, negative thinking & catastrophising

"Once you replace negative thoughts with positive ones, you'll start having positive results." Willie Nelson

Counting- Counting either out loud or in your head. I suggest counting to 10. I find this really comforting in a state of panic or if I feel myself becoming irritated. It brings distraction to any overpowering thoughts as you shift your focus to concentrate on the counting. Remember to count slowly and at a steady pace. If you need to do it more than once, then that is also fine. I often do this exercise a couple of times.

Practice positive self-talk- Be kind to yourself here because being hard on yourself is really not going to improve your current state. Please look over the self-talk page again if you find yourself struggling with this one. It, like anything else, takes practice. Practice self-talk wherever and whenever you can for a calm and positive mind-set.

Mantra's- The word *Mantra* originally used in Hinduism and Buddhism, means to repeat a phase or collection of words to aid the concentration during meditation. Mantra's can also be used outside of meditation at any time. You simply think of a mantra that will be helpful in your current circumstance and repeat it over and over again. Either out loud or in your head it is entirely up to you. Personally, I feel it is more effective when said out loud but if you are out and about this is not always do-able. However you choose to say it, just make sure you repeat it and repeat it. Not only does it provide you encouragement in whatever you are doing, it drowns out any negative thoughts that may creep into your mind in the meantime. A mantra is often better when it is something simple, for example, I can do this. It can really be anything you like; you can get creative with this and see it as an opportunity to tailor something personal. One of my personal mantras is "Kindness does not require a qualification". This is personal to me because whilst studying I sometimes look at the long road ahead which is daunting as it will take a while for me to get to where I want to be. But where do I want to be? I don't have the specifics in my plan as yet; all I know is I want to help people. So "Kindness does not require a qualification" is something I mantra in my head whenever I feel overwhelmed by my studies.

Meditation- Meditation is used to calm and clear the mind. It is a relaxed state in which you channel your thoughts into focusing on a centered single purpose. It is used to silence outside thoughts and enables a tranquil state of mind. Meditation for me has been truly rewarding. I once used to think of meditation as a dull and uninteresting activity. I also thought that you need to be mastered in the art of meditation to find the peace it has to offer. These are certainly not true. Anyone can meditate regardless of ability. I have come to discover that meditation can be used anywhere and for anything. My favourite times to meditate are when I'm hugging my little one to sleep and as preparation before my own sleep. Although there are times where I have found myself meditating on the bus or whilst going for a walk. Meditation sort of flows through, your centered thought is more of a feeling running throughout your body. This brings great warmth and contentment. For instance, If you choose to meditate on the idea of compassion, think about compassion, think about how compassion feels when you receive it, when you give it, feel it not only in your mind but everywhere. Feel it inside your mind, feel it in your heart space, feel it throughout your body and feel it all around you.

Guided meditation is great for beginners because it does what it says, guides you. Through guided meditation you can adjust your breathing, gradually clear out your mind before focusing on the theme of the meditation. This is how I first discovered meditation. I simply typed into YouTube, guided meditation for anxiety, where I found many.

Budda was asked, what have you gained from meditation? He replied, Nothing! However, let me tell you what I have lost: Anger, Anxiety, Depression, Insecurity, Fear of old age and death.

Techniques for staying focused on a positive mentality

"The little things? The little moments? They aren't little." Jon Kabat-Zinn

Here are some techniques I use to keep my minds positive mentality going throughout the day. You don't just have to use them as coping techniques. You can use these techniques whenever and wherever throughout your day to keep a focused positive mentality. I indulge in these experiences making sure I enjoy them every day because they work to keep me calm and focused. You may have personal things you could add to your own list. For example, I find baking, reading and gardening therapeutic.

Observation- Observation can be very calming. It gives you the opportunity to bring peace to the moment you are in. I once mentioned observation to a friend of mine and their response was to ask if I meant 'people watching'. This isn't exactly my take on observation however watching people you love can be of use. I don't mean to sit and stare at your family member whilst they are having a cup of tea. It's more about finding the right moments to observe. Finding these moments are like a blink of happiness. By observing them we can take them in, feel happy in the moment and almost feel like were extracting all the goodness out of it. These moments could be when your child is taking their first steps, your grandparents are laughing together or the anticipation of meeting a friend and hugging them on arrival after you haven't seen them in a while. The smile from your partner as they walk through the door from work, when you're watching your new-born baby sleep in your arms or the warm atmosphere as all the family are gathered around one table for Christmas dinner. These moments are brief and if you blink then you will miss them. Slow yourself down and take the time to relish in these experiences.

-Another type of observation is with nature. Nature can offer us a tranquil earthly experience. Nature is so beautiful but how often do you stop to admire it unless you're in an obviously beautiful location? I am a huge lover of the waves crashing onto the shore, the countryside stretching as far as the eye can see or a gentle stream with clear waters. Although it's not often I see these beautiful places due to the location of where I live. So, I began to look for other less obvious things. I watch the plants and trees surrounding my house and notice how they change not only seasonally but daily too. Take a tree for instance, maybe raindrops are upon the leaves from the rain of the previous day or maybe a spider has cast its web from a branch to several other branches. If you see the same tree every day and yet it appears the same, it is because you are not looking hard enough.

Another thing we can observe is the sky. I personally love to look at the sky. It is always changing. Sometimes the clouds are constantly changing forms, sometimes rainbows stunningly spread across a sky or maybe there is a beautiful clear blue sky. The way that dark stormy clouds can somewhat create almost a shadowy effect and we can observe the world in a different colour. Just like a photographer would change the lighting to obtain their desired effect. We can view the world in colour, in so many different ways. We can enjoy the breath-taking stars that are perfectly present in the sea of the black night sky and the moon which is continuously cycling its various shapes. The orange sky as you watch the sun rise or set in the evening, the sky really is something remarkable in my opinion.

The weather can also be a great thing to observe. Many love a beautiful summer day but find a rainy day dark and depressing. There is actually a condition in which a person's mental mood can shift due to the weather and these people find summer more manageable than winter. I have often experienced my own mood change due to the weather. Have you ever simply stopped to observe the rain before rushing to get out of it? The rain can be so soothing and create a tranquil state within us. The gentle splash as the rain hits the ground and the ripples it causes as a result. Not only is the rain a visual experience. The sound and sensations of the rain are also worth experiencing. The continuous pitter-patter, pitter-patter, pitter-patter as the rain continues to pour. The touch as it falls down and brushes your skin. It's all about a sensory experience you are trying to obtain from it which will fill you with a sense of calm and comfort. When we do this, it allows us to observe the weather from a more positive perspective instead of allowing it to shift us into that dull and depressive mentality.

Sensory- Just like the sensory experience of the above example with the rain we can find comfort in other sensory experiences. These can be with everyday things however the key with sensory experiences is not just to live them but embrace them on every sensory level. There are some conflicting opinions on these types of techniques. Some people love them while some people are not so keen. Maybe you could try one for yourself and see how you feel about it. There is no pressure to enjoy them however personally I really do enjoy my sensory experiences. Although there are many ways to indulge in sensory experiences, I like to incorporate them into my everyday life, so they are easier to enjoy. Here are couple I use if you need some inspiration:

Bath Sensory

This is one of my favourites! I light a few candles to create a glowing ambience. I watch the flicker of the candle and this is soothing. I use coloured bath bombs and watch as they crumble and the colours spread across the water. I love to listen to that gentle fizzing noise as they go. I add various lotions and potions to the water. Some are there to make the water feel silkier, some are there to add some bubbles and the others are there to produce a soothing aroma. I then emerge myself into the bath water and relax. Sometimes I put some therapeutic music on low in the background and read a good book. Other times I use the time to meditate.

-Food Sensory

This one may seem a little odd but the experience is one to relish in. Preferably, this one would work better when you are alone so if you eat with the family at mealtimes you may want to save this one for when you have a cheeky snack. Anticipate your chosen food, look forward to it and feel yourself wanting it more and more. When you come to prepare the food then do this slowly. You are not having a rushed meal or a grab and go snack here. You are trying to slow yourself down so you can relax and enjoy the process. Maybe you want to feel the texture of the food. If you are making something like a sandwich you may want to feel the texture of the bread. Inhale the smell of the bread and then inhale the smell of the filling too. Watch as you spread the butter slowly with the knife and then cut into it. When you have prepared the food, you may want to sit down comfortably to eat it. Before you take a bite though, try to feel the bread or whatever it is as it touches your lips. Take a bite and let it sit on your tongue before you start to chew. When you begin to chew, again, do this slowly, savour the food. Listen as you hear yourself chew and swallow. Take comfort in the repetitive motion of it and delight in its taste. (I told you it was an odd one!)

-Bedtime Sensory

Another one of my favourites! Sometimes it feels like there is no better feeling at the end of a long day as when you climb into bed and pull the covers up. Then you sit or lie in bed and breathe a sigh of relief as you let your body lighten and fall. The moment is a sweet one but a short one. This sensory is all about making the most of this moment. So, before you get into bed make sure your beds made and all ready for you to unwrap. You may wish to light some incense or burn some aroma oils about half an hour before you go to bed. Just please be aware when doing this and make sure they are in a safe place. I do not recommend lighting candles or oil burners as you get into bed as you may fall asleep before you have the chance to put them out. Choose your preferred lighting. You may want lights out or you may prefer a slight glow. I have mood lighting which is basically a light that projects different colours. These colours can be set to gradually fade into one another on loop or set to one preferred colour. Play some relaxation music in the background to add to the tranquil atmosphere and of course wear some comfy warm clothes or pajamas. As you approach the bed take any footware or socks off, so you are barefoot and sit down on the bed. Place your feet onto the carpet and feel the texture on your feet and toes. If you have wooden or titled floors, then you could always use a soft rug or blanket. As you sit place your hands onto the bed and run them over the sheets. You could notice how they feel and take comfort in the niceties of your surroundings. Here would be a perfect time to practice gratitude's. We will look at these a little later in the book but it's really just about being grateful that you have these comforts available to you. You then may want to peel the covers back slowly. When we move slowly it helps to slow our minds down also. As you lay back you can feel your head as it touches the pillow and notice how this makes you feel. As you let your head go, then your arms and legs and eventually your entire body. You let them go and you feel so much lighter. You can practice breathing techniques here and use them to welcome calmness not only to your physical body but to your mind. You may want to drift off to sleep by using a sleep meditation, some therapeutic sleep music or an audio story.

Music- I think everyone can feel a connection to music. It's powerful, in ways that can change your mood instantly and bring emotions to the surface. Using music as a positive tool is invaluable. Providing that you listen to the right empowering and uplifting music. Although, with this being said, there is nothing wrong with listening to music that can bring

upsetting emotions to the surface because it is always helpful to let these emotions out instead of keeping them in. I always find the time, usually once a week, to allow myself some emotional release through music. The main thing to add here is that although it is an important thing to do, it is also an important thing is you are able to keep yourself safe while doing this and to bring yourself out of this emotional state afterwards. I suggest finding a balance. Listen to music that will help release your emotions and then equally listen to music that will brighten your mood again at the end. Of course, you can just listen to uplifting music whenever you like, it's such a magical and rewarding experience to give yourself.
Personally, I love songs where I can relate to the lyrics. It gives me a sense of knowing I am not alone, and it also reminds me of how far I've come. One of my favorite bands is- Icon for Hire. Their songs have helped me through some of my darkest times and really marked the start of my transitional journey to a better version of myself. The first song I ever heard from them is called- Supposed to be. It really summed up how I was feeling at the time. I had recently received my diagnosis of BPD and I knew there was changes that I had to make but somehow by conquering the illness I wasn't entirely sure of who I was. I knew I needed to find my identity and start discovering who I was supposed to be. Listening to the song now, although it isn't really still relevant, it reminds me of how far I've come and that I am proud of myself for overcoming this. I'd also like to share another song, it has also been helpful for me on my journey- Tonight Alive: World away. This song helped me over the massive uphill struggle that was my driving test. It's one of the hardest things I've done because I was such an anxious driver!

Journaling- Journaling can be a useful way of reflecting on your life's events and experiences. Everybody has their ups and downs but being able to record and reflect on these can really help to improve things going forward. If something hasn't gone to plan you can take the time to process this and learn where you went wrong and try to do things differently next time around. Positivity is also good to reflect on, harness these good moments, don't just write them down but write how they made you feel. It can be nice to try recapture these feelings when you read what you've written at a later date. Journaling also allows you to release any worries, doubts or negative emotions you have by writing them down on paper. In doing so you are releasing them from your mind and creating space for calm and positive thoughts to enter instead.

Earthing- I won't go into too much detail about earthing as it's not for everyone. Google 'earthing' and it will bring up all you need to know. Earthing is drawing natural energy from and connecting you to the earth. Tree hugging is particularly helpful in increasing oxytocin levels and releases serotonin and dopamine hormones which make you feel happier. Earthing offers a holistic approach to healing.

Taking Back Control- BPD

Taking Back Control- BPD

Chapter 3:
Creative Expressive Arts

"There's no such thing as creative people and non-creative people. There are only people who use their creativity and people who don't." Brené Brown

What is Creative Expressive Arts (CEA)?

CEA is a creative expression through the discovery and creativity of the arts. It is used within therapies to bring emotions to the surface, relieving the individual of emotional distress and start a healing process. It's also great in the fact that it provides a good distraction from the outside world and is a therapeutic experience. It's seen as a healthy and safe way to explore emotions. Although creative expression is form of therapy it can just as easily be done without a therapist and you don't have to be an artist. It's a personal experience where you are free to express your emotions through the arts in whichever way you desire. CEA are a great way to express, reflect, experience and self-discover on your journey of healing. Plus, it can also be a lot of fun!!!

There are some various example types of CEA:

- Visual Art
- Drama
- Music
- Movement
- Writing

Taking Back Control- BPD

Here are some useful CEA suggestions:

- Photography
- Free writing
- Positive patterns
- Free spirited scribble
- Painting
- Drawing
- Adult colouring
- Scrapbooking
- Collages
- Photo/Memory book
- Vision Board
- Singing
- Dancing
- Acting/Performing
- Song Writing/Music writing
- Creative hobbies (Knitting, cardmaking etc.)
- Playing a musical instrument
- Letters
- Poetry

I'm sure there is probably loads more as there are so many ways to creatively express ourselves... but you get the idea!

How has CEA helped me?

Personally, CEA has helped me to heal over time by providing a creative outlet for me to able to express emotions safely. Here is a vision board I created at the start of 2020.

Community Art

I wanted this book to capture community diversity and share real community creative expressive arts. Thank you to all that have shared their artwork or poetry. I hope you enjoy looking through the community art submissions and that they are relatable and inspiring for you.

Such is my fortune

A book of individual poetry-by A.C. Holloway & Jennifer. S. F. Raynor.

This collection of poems is written by members of the mental health community. The project aims to reveal the person under the mental health label.

You can purchase 'Such is my fortune' from Amazon.co.uk

Taking Back Control- BPD

'Milky Way Sky'

Attributed to Ashley Ferrari & Enchanted Fantasy Art.

Creative expressive arts have helped me to better manage my emotions and to replace some unhealthy coping mechanisms. They enable me to create my own beauty in a world that often feels dark. While painting I feel a sense of peace and serenity, feelings I aim to pass on to the viewer.

Taking Back Control - BPD

BPD Artwork

By Pippa Nayer

Fighting the stigma - overcoming negative stories and replacing them with love

Taking Back Control- BPD

Carrie Raven- Artwork collection

Looking back at the art I have made, as though a journal, I am able to reconnect to the moments associated with each artwork; I am sometimes provided a stable context to my life and a grounding in my reality

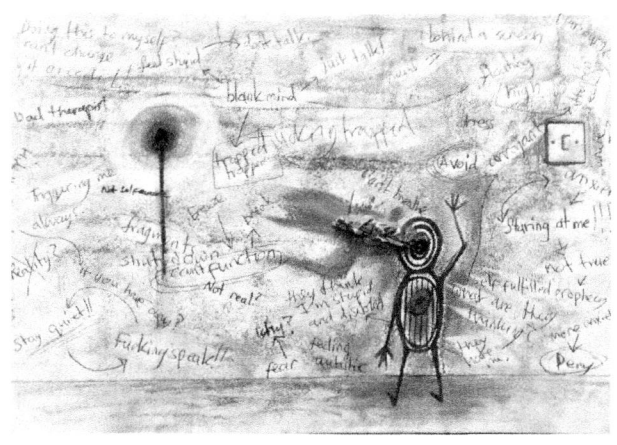

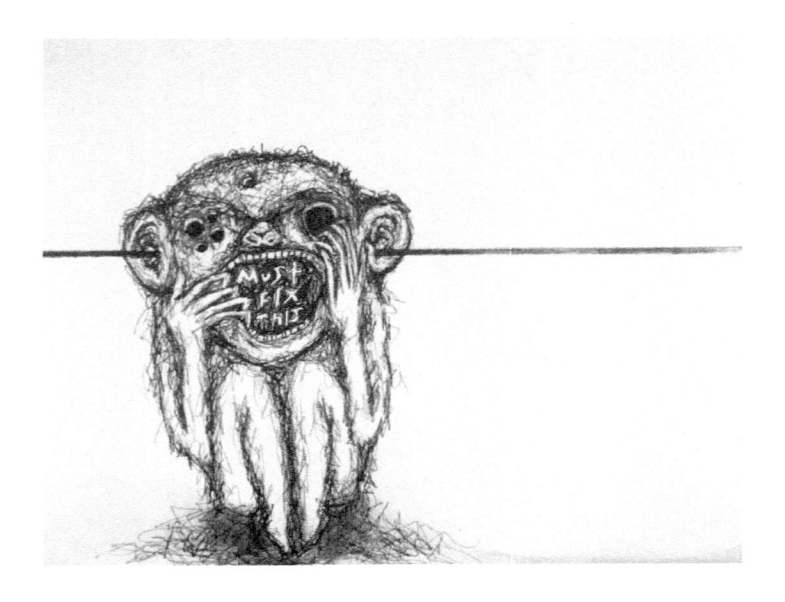

Taking Back Control- BPD

Taking Back Control- BPD

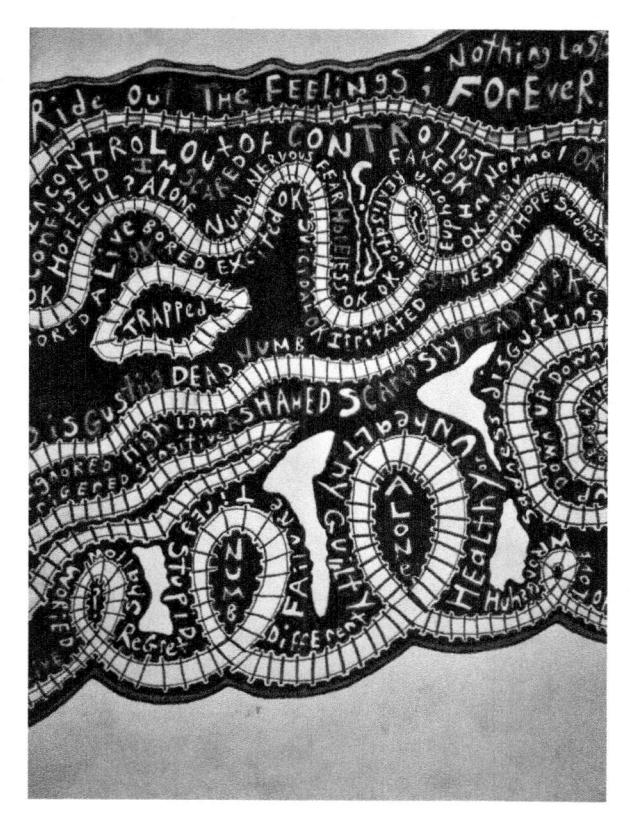

Taking Back Control- BPD

Bethan Downs- Dancer

Bethan is a dancer and has shared her accounts of what it means to her. She has over 20 years of experience and is well-versed in many dance styles.

I started dance around the age of 3, so 20plus years I've been dancing. I've trained in many styles from Ballet, Tap, Contemporary, Jazz, Modern, Latin, freestyle, Ballroom, Lyrical to street/urban and a few other styles.

Over the years I've been able to perform in many shows, I've been lucky enough to perform at Royal Albert hall four times, and Portaventure Salou in Spain and these both were with Mardi Gras.

I love dancing, not only because you can enjoy making new friends, but you can tell a story through your performance. My favourite style is Ballet, being able to dance on pointe is beautiful, and a tiny bit painful, but I love it.

I've had many opportunities over the years to dance with professional choreographers in workshops and to do meet and greets with Professional choreographers. I love watching all sorts of dance programmes, my favourite has to be strictly come dancing. You can see that the celebrities are enjoying themselves. If it weren't for my parents taking me to dance class, I have no idea what I'd have done. I wouldn't have had the opportunities to perform in the places I've performed at or meet Professional choreographers.

When a good song comes on, I just want to dance, or when an old song comes which I've danced to I try to remember the dance. I've had so many good times and funny times too. I remember in a 1940's weekend in my hometown, at the brewers my dance school did a performance. I only went and turned the wrong way to the rest of them and ended up stood on my own, but I just turned towards them and carried on. I'm not sure if many noticed but I know my parents did and they haven't let me forget. Every time we hear the song play somewhere, they just look at me and we all laugh. I also remember the time I was in a show, I ran off the back wing and fell over a speaker, that didn't half hurt! It went the quiet and you could hear the whole audience gasp.

I don't go to dance class much now, because of working full time, but I still love to make up choreography and dance around in the living room! In dance, you can tell a story, you can express how you feel when creating dances. Whether this be love, scared, sad or whatever else you choose. It's about the way you move and the emotion you put into it. Also, finding the right song too... that helps a lot!

For more Creative Expressive Arts subscribe to taking back controls YouTube channel:
https://www.youtube.com/channel/UCxsukqEGeYAatFdcJHkyy9A

If you would like to share your Creative Expressive Arts, get in touch by emailing me at: takingbackcontroleupd@gmail.com

Taking Back Control- BPD

> *"Poetry is when an emotion has found it's thoughts and the thought has found words."* Robert Frost

Life on paper

Written By Emma Warren
(Pre-diagnosis aged 20)

Try read me like a book,
I warn you now,
you won't have much luck.
Things aren't always as they appear,
in my mind I'm hidden away,
and that's what I fear.
At work in my head,
I scream and shout,
"STOP OBSERVING ME!"
I need to get out.

The need to run,
the need to hide,
to stop the voices inside.
They won't stop,
they just keep coming,
and that is why,
I keep on running.

I know you don't see it,
but you must understand,
I'm stuck with it now,
not like it was planned.
Don't know how it started,
or how it will end,
to you I look normal,
that's how I pretend.

I am here,
please don't make me shout,
in a room full of people,
don't let me fade out,
I look in a mirror,
just stand and stare,
it's a faded image,
of what once was there.

In front of you,
I will try not to cry,
but the tears just fall,
escaped from inside.
Breathe and breathe,
I am not on show,
find a safe place,
so you'll never know.

The words they hurt,
just think what you say,
they haunt my dreams,
each night and day.
I see my life,

Taking Back Control- BPD

go past my eyes,
things I would change,
but they've had their time.

If you are around,
I will always try avoid,
don't think I'm being rude,
don't be annoyed.
I feel under-pressure,
pushed into a space,
just want to get away,
so I can bury my face.

Just make it go away,
don't wanna do it anymore,
feels like I'm falling,
I'll soon hit the floor.
Talk to a brick wall,
you never seem to hear,
I fear I will lose,
all the things I hold dear.

How do I sit,
and what do I say,
things I must overcome,
and deal with every day.
The things I lock up,
they must stay hidden,
to speak them out loud,
is completely forbidden.

So scared that my secrets,
will be conversed,
don't make a fuss,
it will only make it worse.
Don't treat me differently,
I'm just like you,
I bet that deep down,
you have your own problems too.

Negative thoughts,
run through my brain,
word by word,
they drive me insane.
The rage kept inside,
where people can't see,
I want to scream and scream,
won't it just let me be.

Get out of my mind,
stay out of my head,
over and over,
these words are said.
They never leave me alone,
so I will never succeed,
but I keep on running,
and wish to be freed.

Taking Back Control- BPD

Chapter 4: Self-doubt VS Self-belief

"It's not what you are that holds you back, it's what you think you are

not." Denis Waitley

Taking Back Control- BPD

Comparison

Have you ever felt like you're not good enough for this world?

Have you ever thought... why doesn't anything ever go my way?

Have you ever felt like everything seems to be a challenge and you never get anywhere?

You're hitting brick walls everywhere you turn and no one else seems to understand. You feel stuck in a never-ending cycle of never being able to make things go your way. You're sick and tired of feeling buried under by the expectations of society. You feel like the grass is ALWAYS greener on the side. You find yourself comparing yourself to everyone around you and thinking I'll never match up. Feeling like you're ten steps behind trying to play catch up.

You're chasing and chasing and chasing!

Want to know how to catch up?

The answer is simple, although not what you might expect.

The answer is to simply STOP... Stop chasing!

When we compare ourselves against others, we are setting ourselves up to fail. We're not failing because we can't catch up, we are failing because we take away our ability to see were chasing in the wrong direction. Comparing ourselves against others can be destructive. When we compare, we often see the best in others and see the worst in ourselves. We are constantly feeding our self-doubt based on the guidelines that have been set by others. We result in believing that we are different and see it as a bad thing. We lose all confidence, all motivation and all pride in our abilities. We can often end up resenting others for their success in comparison to our own. It's no wonder that we want to curl up in ball, pretend they don't exist and stop trying altogether.

We can never measure ourselves by other people's successes; we can only measure ourselves against our own successes. Every single one of us is different and we all have different things to offer. Comparing yourself against someone else is like comparing an apple to a chocolate bar. They are two very different things and whilst some may argue that apples are healthier for us, others will argue that their chocolate bar just can't be beaten on taste regardless of the fat content. Some people prefer to eat an apple whilst some people will always opt for the chocolate bar. Essentially, there is no wrong decision and it's down to your own personal preference. Measuring ourselves against others is very much like this. Some people will prefer your method to do something whilst others will prefer someone else's method. If both methods work and have the same outcome does it really matter what method people choose to get themselves there?

Take an exam for instance, you've tired your very best, given it your all and you get 43 out of 50. Your friend on the other hand gets 49 out of 50. Automatically you go to a place of thinking I wasn't good enough because I scored less than my friend. Now consider if you had taken the exam and your friend hadn't. You would have no other score to compare yours against. Would you then think that actually 43 out of 50 is very good and find satisfaction in it? I'm willing to bet that most people would. Take your friend out of the picture regardless of whether they also took the exam or not as that does not matter here. You scored 43 out of 50 however in your last exam you only scored 37 out of 50. Compare yourself against your own scores and you will have learned that you have improved so you are obviously doing something right.

If you're going to compete against someone then compete against yourself. Not only does it inspire your growth, but you will also feel satisfied from doing something right instead of viewing it as something wrong. If you achieve less than the last time you may want to rethink your approach. Maybe you need to do a little more research, to dedicate more time or to try something different. There is always something to learn from yourself. If you are achieving less, it's an obvious signal that you need to reassess and make some changes.

If you're going to continue to compare yourself against others, then I'm sorry to say that you will always be playing catch up. There is always going to be someone out there that you will perceive as 'better' than yourself. Please remember the fact that no one is ever perfect, remember that we are all of different abilities and while you may lack in one area you are mastered in another. Above all though, enjoy the process of measuring yourself against your own measurements. Isn't it exciting to be able to learn and grow? If we had nothing to learn, don't you think life would get very boring, very quickly? Learning and growing are so important otherwise what would be the point?!

Rejection

Rejection can play a big part in keeping our self-doubt at the forefront of our minds. The impact of rejection forces us to confirm our own self-doubtful thoughts and feelings. Believe it or not rejection is a healthy process on our journey to self-belief. It all comes down to that recurring theme of that word 'perspective'.

How are you choosing to take on your rejections?

Are you using them to fuel your self-doubt or using them to inspire change?

There is so much to learn from our rejections and yet we choose to ignore these teachings and give in entirely. If you get rejected one hundred times, what have you learnt from these rejections? Nothing? No way! You'll find that you have learned one hundred ways of how not to do something. Now, I am not saying that being rejected one hundred times is easy to take, in fact far from it, but does it give you less hope each time? Or does it strengthen your resilience each time you get back up and try again? Rejection requires A LOT of patience and determination. It is something I've personally found one of the hardest things to be able to overcome. It is so powerful in taking away your self-confidence and self-esteem. It's like it takes over and drives you on autopilot down the road of self-doubt. So many people are letting it take control and do not know how take the wheel and steer the other way again.

Rejection can present itself in many forms big or small. For instance, if you have asked your friend to hang out at the weekend and your friend responds with '*Sorry but I think I'll be hanging out with another friend this weekend*'.

How do you choose to internalise this response?
Do you feel rejected by your friend?
Do you suddenly find yourself heading down a downward spiral?
What does this person have that I don't?
What have I done wrong?
Has my friend grown tired of my friendship, are they leaving me behind while they make other friends? The spiral may continue downwards until you find yourself harbouring some resentment towards your friend. You find yourself thinking things like, well fine, I have better things to do than hang out with you anyway. I'll ask someone else who isn't going to turn me down. I won't be making the effort to ask again; they will have to ask me now.

Before you know it, you've gone off the original idea altogether and resulted in some bitterness towards your friend. You're left feeling deflated and let down and wonder why you even bothered asking in the first place. This can be the sort of downward spiral you find yourself going down with any sort of rejection, whether something little like the friend example or something a little bigger. Maybe you've been rejected for a job. Maybe you've asked someone out for a drink, but they have refused. Maybe it's something bigger than this. Maybe you've just found out your husband or wife has been cheating on you. Maybe your teenage child is refusing to listen to anything you have to say and has decided they no longer need you. Feeling rejected is indeed a part of life whether big or small.

Unfortunately, pain is part of the process of rejection. Rejection can be brutal and cruel in the first instance, almost so that you are reluctant to accept it. An old friend of mine once used the phrase 'Time is a healer and patience is your friend' these words could not be truer for reluctance. Do not feel alarmed if you can't accept your rejection head on and up front. Some things take time to digest. We have a processing filter that allows us to filter things through at an emotionally tolerable pace. There is no time limit on this, and it should not be forced. Trust in your process filter. When you are ready to accept your rejection then this is what you must do, accept it. By allowing yourself time to process the matter you will be able to accept it. I'm not saying you'll miraculously feel better on the matter, but you will feel lighter with your acceptance.

Take a look at the diagram:

SELF-BELIEF

←You are here

SELF-DOUBT

The diagram is a representation of your self-doubt vs your self-belief. Wherever you may feel you are on the ladder at this current time we are going to start in the middle. You're in the neutral zone.

Let's take the example of a job rejection, one of many.

You applied yourself, put your best efforts into your application and job interview. You honestly believe you have made a really good impression. You feel hopeful but also doubtful- worrying that you were not as good as the other applicants. Then you receive a telephone call, you realise it is from the company you applied with and that they were ringing to let you know the outcome. They are sorry to inform you that you have not been successful this time.

Your heart sinks... You can feel like your small wall of hope is crumbling down inside you. You confirm to yourself all those doubtful things you had felt previous to the outcome. On the one hand you feel like you could cry and feel pity for yourself as you've been rejected yet again. On the other hand, you feel an anger growing inside you. You're angry at yourself, the company and the world in general for handing you rejection time and time again.

You muster up a response whilst on the phone. You express gratitude for the opportunity although you are not feeling wholesome in this gratitude. You take the time to ask for some feedback. As you hear the feedback you are really feeling that you had not done as well as you originally thought. You realise that they have been deeply negative in pointing out all the things that you could have improved on whilst the positive feedback was lacking. All positive feedback was diminished when they continued to say things like 'you answered the questions very well, but you took a little too long to think of the answers' every positive being undermined by a negative. You thank them once again before ending the phone call. As you hang up you feel deflated and overwhelmed with a sense of failure. You find yourself thinking statements like 'I'll never be good enough', 'Why do I never catch a break' and 'The world hates me for some reason and I hate the world'.

Starting to sound familiar?

Believe me when I say that I know this feeling all too well. My self-doubt was on the floor for a very, very long time. I started to become numb to rejections after so long and figured well I'm not worthy of anything better. I didn't have any hope left for it to break down and I expected anything and everything bad that could happen to me to happen. It became easier to believe that I was going to fail or be rejected because then I wouldn't have anything left to lose or anything to feel worse about when it happened. This is a dark, depressive and seriously unhealthy hole to be stuck in.

So how do you get out of this hole?

How do move up your ladder of self-doubt VS self-belief?

The first step is to take responsibility. Now to take responsibility this does not mean that you blame yourself for your shortcomings. It's about owning your rejections, learning to accept them and giving power to your strengths. You need to take back control and recognise that this is not the end of the world. The world will continue go on around you whether you choose to move with it or without it.

You need to find perspective in the matter. Ask yourself what you would say to a friend who was in the same position. As an outsider you are more able to see the issue for what it is and give positive support to your friend. Although you may sympathise with your friend you are not bogged down by the same emotional state or clouded mentality. You recognise that they are going through a hard time, but you also know that this will not always be the case. You trust that they will be turning the situation around and be feeling better soon. You are in a better position to see their situation clearly. It is certainly easier to gain perspective of your friend's position but not necessarily your own. We doubt ourselves continuously and do not trust in our own abilities to change the situation the way we trust our friends to.

We need to break out of the limiting capacity we give ourselves. We need to believe that we, just like our friends, are capable of taking control. Ultimately if you don't take responsibility then no one else will. There is no knight in shining armour ready to swoop down and say: 'Don't worry about the recent job rejection. You've been rejected so many times I'm going to give you a job now.' No one is going to change this for us, only we can do that and only we have responsibility over our own lives. Once we decide to take responsibility, we let go of the victim mentality.

After you've decided to take responsibility and hopefully gained a little perspective. You are in a much better position to be able to accept. Accepting is the next part of the process. You need to accept that you have not got the job. Be very mindful of your self-talk and try to accept with ease and understanding. Only when we take responsibility and learn to accept can we then start to make the changes to improve our self-belief.

Now at the moment you are still in the middle of the ladder and you will find, along with many other things in this book, that you have choice.

Are you going to move down the ladder and continue to feed your self-doubt?

Or are you going to make a stand?

Are you going to grab the reins and take back control and move up the ladder?
The ball is in your court and you can play this however you choose. Take a moment right now... recognise how you are feeling... do you subconsciously doubt your ability to take back control as you read this? Self-doubt can always be

lingering when we don't even realise it. We need to drown the self-doubt out and we need to find that little bit of self-belief in ourselves and squeeze it dry. You can turn your rejections into positives. Take a hold of the self-belief and really harness all those good, positive and hopeful feelings. You can move up the ladder, you can do it, believe you can do it.

Still not convinced?

Let's take a look at what might be holding you back...

Stuck in the past

Are past mistakes and experiences holding you back?

It's understandable if things have not gone quite to plan in the past. There can be many little things or there can be a bigger thing that is taking centre in the forefront of your mind. We often bury our head in the sand and choose to ignore these. By choosing to do this we aren't letting them go in the way we need, we are subconsciously holding on them and using them to determine our current experiences.

It's important to learn from our past mistakes and experiences, this is how we grow and how we improve. However, if you haven't realised it by now we need to use these in a controlled way. In other words, we need to decipher what we can take from these past experiences that are going to help us and what will not. It may take you some time to sift through your past experiences and determine what is of help and what is not. I suggest you start with your most fore minded experience. Choose the experience that always comes to mind when you remind yourself of how it didn't quite go to plan that time. As you go through many new experiences then others may arise. I recommend doing these as they come to mind so you're only dealing with one thing at a time.

Think of your chosen past experience and try to think of how you felt. Make a table like the one below and list the thoughts/feelings that arise down the left column. The right column will be used to list the things we are going to take from the situation or leave behind.

As an example, I have used one of my personal past experiences. At this time, I was working in a

Taking Back Control- BPD

supermarket and failing my staff standards report month after month. A staff standards report is something my supervisor would fill out each month to pick out any areas that needed improvement. Needless to say, I needed work on every area, every single month, there was never any improvement. Notice in my example when I move to another job, I use my past experience to predict the outcome.

Unhelpful	Helpful
I felt embarrassed. I'll only embarrass myself again.	I choose to leave my embarrassment behind. It shows that I felt judged by others. I refuse to let unproven judgement from others determine the way I will perform again.
I could not improve then so why would it be any different now?	I found it difficult to improve back then because I was in an unhealthy abusive relationship. This understandably impacted my performance at work. Now I'm in a better place and I trust in my abilities to move forward.
Trying does not get me anywhere.	Actually, trying gets me everywhere if I choose to see it this way. There is always something to learn, especially from my mistakes. I choose to try and learn.
I'm a failure, I was then, and I am now.	The actual definition of failure is- A lack of success. The definition is not- Give up... that's the end. However, I do choose to end being a failure and start being a success. Who I was then is not who I am now or who I will be in the future.
I will never be good enough for a job.	What's good enough anyway? I choose to leave this mentality behind and take forward a mentality that is keen to learn and motivated to grow.
There's something wrong with me.	I choose to leave the impression of myself as being wrong in the past. Instead, I figure I may be different to others around me but who's normal anyway? I am different, I am unique,

Overall, from this exercise I learned that I needed to forgive myself for this not so good experience. I was doing the best I could at that time of my life. I realise that now I am in a better place and who I am now is different to the person I was back then. I accept the challenge of trying to work again knowing that I'll handle anything that I need to. I feel excited with the understanding that I can bring something unique to my position.

Have a go at the exercise yourself, it can be for anything you feel that may be holding you back from taking on something new in your life. Repeat the process as much or as little as you need. By repeating the process, we teach ourselves to change our perspective from the onset and you will find yourself forgetting the negatives and replacing them with positives.

Repeat, practice and choose a positive mentality.

Feel the fear & do it anyway- Susan Jeffers

Feel the fear and do it anyway (Susan Jeffers, 1987, feel the fear and do it anyway), a book that comes highly recommended. It talks about why we fear things and how to overcome these fears. I wanted to include this for you because the quote/title alone has helped me on numerous occasions.

The point is that there will always be fear, the fear is unavoidable, but you know what?
Just do it anyway!
Why not?
What do you have to lose?
And what are you gaining by not doing it?
A big question for me was- What if I do it anyway and fail?

My fear was failing but what I could not see was, that choosing not to do something because I was afraid, was failing me anyway. It was failing me because I never gave myself the chance to succeed at anything. Yes, I might fail but equally so I might succeed. It certainly crossed my mind when I was wondering whether I should write this book. Sometimes I would think, it'll never be good enough, no one will read it, or no one would take me seriously. After reading *'Feel The Fear And Do It Anyway'*, I thought, 'well what if my book is good enough? What if many people do read it? And what if they took me seriously and changed their lives because of something I had written?' What a great opportunity with a chance of success. Was I going to pass up that opportunity and forever doubt the worth of my ideas? All of sudden, the not doing it had raised fear instead. I didn't want to regret not taking the chance.

Yes... I still felt fear, but I did it anyway!

Exercise (word replacement)

Here is another exercise you might like to have a go at. It is to do with our self-talk. Self-talk is so important because it gives us control of our thought processing. Simply by changing the way we talk to ourselves in our minds can impact our emotional state.

For instance, if you were to say, I should have gone food shopping today! How do you then feel about that statement? Do you feel guilty that you haven't? Do you feel angry that you should have done it, but you haven't? The question to ask is, why you haven't gone food shopping today? Try and remember your tone here, try asking in a calm and inquisitive manner. Is it simply because you haven't had the time? Is it because you didn't feel like it? Or has it just escaped your mind up until now? Whatever your reason tell yourself, it is okay. The fact that you haven't gone food shopping today isn't going to change, so if you're going to raise the point to yourself about it, then there is no point in beating yourself up over something you cannot change.

Here is the exercise: In the left column you will see the original thought and in the right column I want you to add an alternative thought. How can you change the original thought to a kinder thought? The answers will be useful when you are practicing your self-talk. Being kinder to ourselves gives us more control over the situation. Choose to be kind to yourself and trust that you can change the situation around. You will realise that being harsh on yourself is just unhelpful and unnecessary.

Original	Kind Alternative
I should have	I could have
I can't do it	
I need to be better	
I'm losing control	
I'm failing	
I will never	
I'm not good enough	

In relation to our food shopping example:

I should have gone food shopping today – I could have gone food shopping today.

You could then use the question you answered about why you didn't go to follow your self-talk:

I could have gone food shopping today, but I have had a very busy day and it's okay that I didn't find the time. I could go tomorrow instead as I am free in the morning.

Say goodbye to unhelpful original thoughts because they will not benefit you. Practice your self-talk with kind alternatives and you will feel better. Personally, I felt like I was less under pressure and less under scrutiny from myself. I felt like I was taking back control of my thought patterns and more able to control the situation around me. This is such a simple exercise, but it can make a big difference. Maybe you could think of some more things to add to the list and you may want to put the list somewhere you can see it. I have mine on the fridge and I find seeing it daily helps.

Fake it to make it

Ever heard the term- fake to make it? I lived by this saying for a couple of years until I reached a point where I wasn't actually faking at it anymore. I pretended to be someone who was more confident, more assertive and more in control. I used the word pretend because that's kind of what it was like. I remember discussing it one time at my most recent therapy. I said, it's like I put on this mask when I leave the house and take it off when I come home again. The thing is, that I was using this mask not to change who I was but to be who I was all along. I essentially realised that I can choose the person I want to be and if I make the changes, I will make it real. So, in light of this, I guess you could really refer to the mask as a confidence mask. Heck, why not go all out and say it's a superhero mask. What made it super is that it gave me confidence. What made it heroic is that fact that I chose to put this mask on however scared I felt and go out with pride. In a way, as cheesy as it sounds, I was my own hero. It was scary at first like everything, but *I felt the fear and did it anyway.* Until a time came when I realised, it was not scary anymore and I had not only gotten rid of the mask, but I'd forgotten it altogether. It is within you to be exactly who you desire to be. So, if you doubt yourself at first then be brave and fake it. When you start making it you can start to believe in yourself.

As I have mentioned previously, I had had my own

self-doubt arise in the process of writing this book. I'd mentioned my writing to a couple of people, and when they questioned me about what it was that I was writing, I would freeze. I'd say things like, 'Oh nothing much! Just personal stuff or just something little about what I've learnt'. I doubted myself and so I was reluctant to tell people the truth. Always skirting around the edges and never giving a direct honest answer. I would fear people's opinions and assume that they would take one look at me and say, 'There's no way YOU can write about that'. However, I wanted people to take me seriously, but how were people going to take me seriously if I didn't take myself seriously?

I then decided I was going to run a little experiment. When people would ask me about my 'work', I would answer, "I'm a student but I'm also a writer". I would say that I was a writer, regardless of whether I believed it or not. The response was surprising; most people didn't ask me what I was studying as they originally did, in-fact they didn't ask me anything about my studies. Instead, they eagerly asked, "What is it you write?". I would answer honestly every time and people were so kind and enthusiastic about the book. I didn't receive a single negative comment and I felt like people were being genuine in their responses and not just being polite. As a result, I was finally starting to believe that I AM a writer and that I was proud to be able to tell people that.

Let's take another look at this diagram:

[Diagram: A ladder with "SELF-BELIEF" labeled at the top and "SELF-DOUBT" at the bottom. An arrow in the middle indicates "You are here".]

How do you feel about it now? I understand that self-doubt can often overpower self-belief and you need good hard evidence to power your self-belief. How are you going to get that evidence? You need to take action. You need to believe for a moment that you can, even if you doubt this belief. You need to *'fear the fear and do it anyway'*, you need to **fake it to make it** and you will start to obtain more belief as you go. There will always be things that test you and you will find yourself moving up and down the ladder as they arise. I must express how important it is to always **accept first** and then start in the middle, not the bottom. If you are starting on the floor you are in an almost impossible position to move upwards. Starting in the middle gives you the chance to realise that yes you do have some fear about the situation but at the same time you know that you need to take action to be able to move upwards. Give yourself some time to really put yourself in position where you can move. You don't need to believe at first you just need to want to believe. Be patient and give yourself some credit. The first step is always the hardest.

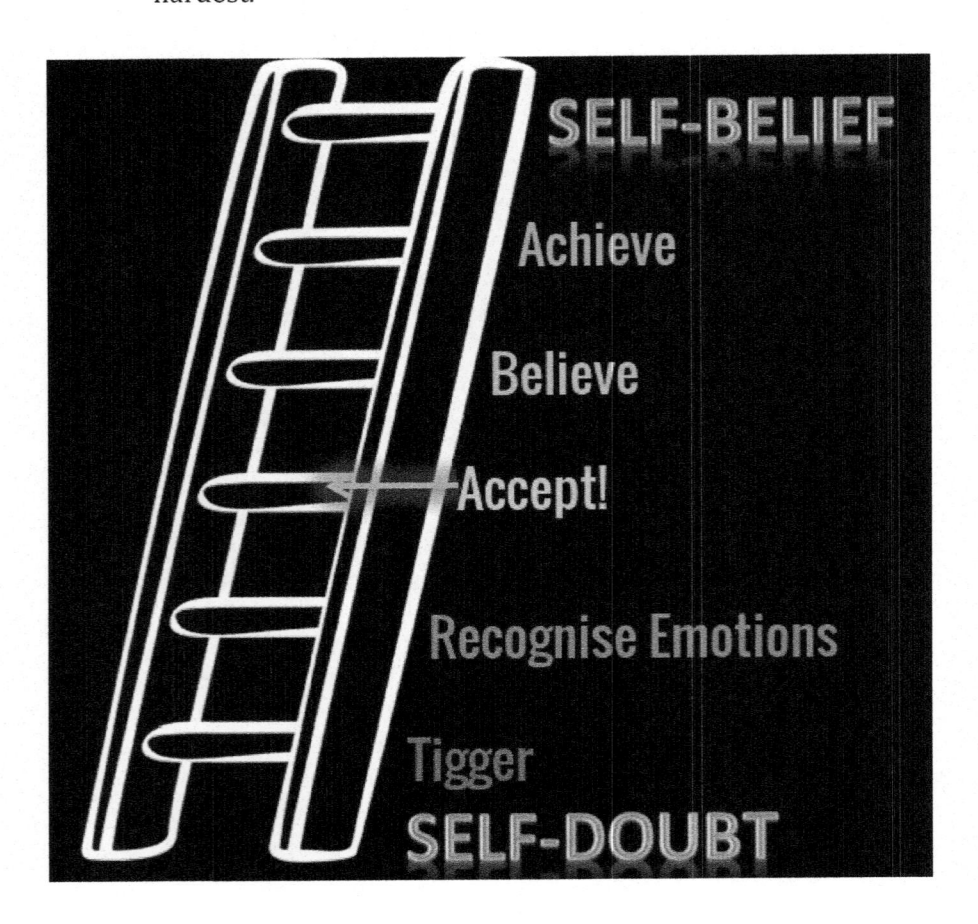

SELF-BELIEF
Achieve
Believe
←—Accept!
Recognise Emotions
Tigger
SELF-DOUBT

Self-doubt VS self-belief is an ongoing process. There are still times I get knocked down a step or two particularly when it comes to rejection. When I realise I've been knocked down, I take responsibility, accept it and move myself up to the middle of the ladder. Then I take action and start to slowly move up again. There is never a fixed point to the ladder and you will find yourself moving up and down continuously. The important point here is that you will not be on the floor or the lower steps for long, you don't have to be stuck again. You can change it and you can take back control.

Afirmations

Affirmations are the act of repeating thoughts that empower you. They are a great way to practice positive thinking and serve as a motivation tool. An affirmation is a statement that is said in the present tense and effectively allows you to affirm to yourself that you can do anything. With affirmations you can choose to write and say your own and this can be more personalised and specific. However, you can find audio tapes, books or audios online also. As I mentioned in the coping techniques for intrusive thoughts section in chapter 2- Self-talk & Coping Techniques.

Here are a few examples:

- I accept the things I cannot change, and I learn from my mistakes.
- I have confidence in myself that I will handle anything that comes my way.
- I believe and trust in myself.
- Today I am reborn, and I plan to use my time wisely and productively.
- I feel enthusiastic and motivated to start my day.
- I choose to focus my thoughts to positive thinking now, the present and leave unhelpful thoughts in the past.
- I am kind, I am kind to myself and I am kind to others.
- I respond to other people's negativity without compromise to my own positivity.

There is a lot to take in from this chapter, but I hope you can take something from it that is helpful.

Let's have a quick recap...

- We should never compare our own successes against other peoples. The only person we should compete against is ourselves.
- Remember that no one is perfect, and everyone has something different to offer, including yourself.
- Learn to take responsibility for your rejections and then accept them in your own time.
- You are responsible for your own life and you can choose to take action.
- Gain perspective of the situation and don't get sucked into the downward spiral of self-doubting.
- Learn to accept or let go of past experiences that do not serve you.
- Choose to learn from your past mistakes but in a controlled way. Only use helpful thoughts.
- *Feel the fear and do it anyway.*
- Practice positive self-talk by using kind alternatives.
- Be brave by using the fake it to make it

approach.

- Take action and gather some evidence for self-belief so you can move up the ladder.

- Even if you feel overwhelmed with self-doubt always remember to start in the middle of your ladder.

- Remember you don't need to believe at first you just need to want to believe.

- Assess how you feel throughout to make sure you're heading in the right direction.

- Use affirmations as a motivational tool and an effective reinforcement for positive thinking.

Taking Back Control- BPD

Chapter 5- Recognising & Managing BPD Emotions

"I'm stronger than you know, cause unbreakable pieces don't shatter, I won't shatter, you can't shatter me now. I'm taking back my life and putting myself back together. I won't shatter, you can't shatter me now. I'm unbreakable!"- New Years Day: Unbreakable (song lyrics)

Part 1: Recognising BPD Emotions

BPD Diagnosis Criteria

According to the DSM- Diagnostic and statistical manual of mental disorders, the current nine criteria of diagnosing BPD are:

1. Frantic efforts to avoid real or imagined abandonment.

2. A pattern of unstable or intense interpersonal relationships categorised by alternating between extremes of idealisation and devaluation.

3. Identity disturbance: Markedly and persistently unstable self-image or sense of self.

4. Impulsivity in at least two areas that are potentially self-damaging.

5. Recurrent suicidal behaviour, gestures, or threats, or self-mutilating behaviour.

6. Affective instability due to a marked reactivity of mood.

7. Chronic feelings of emptiness.

8. Inappropriate, intense anger or difficulty controlling anger.

9. Transient, stress-related paranoid ideation or severe dissociative symptoms.

To be diagnosed with BPD you must be presenting with at least five of the BPD criteria.

What is BPD?

BPD is categorised as a mental personality disorder in which a person has difficulties regulating emotions and controlling impulsions. The behaviour presented by someone with BPD can become apparent as maladaptive methods of coping with constant emotional pain are experienced. Someone with BPD can rapidly fluctuate between patterns of despair and confidence. Along with feelings of choric emptiness and fear of abandonment, self-harm or suicidal thoughts may also be present.

Latest research indicates that BPD is a biologically based disorder of the emotional regulation system, which maybe due to the environment or a combination of these two factors. These biological "vulnerabilities" may place a person at increased risk of developing BPD given certain developmental factors, such as stressful events in the early family environment. It is often that other family members may also experience mental health issues.

BPD patients are arguably the most stigmatised within the mental health system. They very often won't be offered any support for their BPD. Dialectical Behavioral Therapy is the most effect therapy used to treat BPD, although few in the UK are offered this.

BPD is unofficially categorised as either 'Classic BPD' or 'Quiet BPD', although these aren't a separated diagnosis, they are recognised within the BPD community. It's said that a person with 'Classic BPD' express their emotions outwardly, whereas a person with 'Quiet BPD' expresses their emotions inwardly. They both however experience the same levels of emotional intensity. It's an important point to address because I've had people with a BPD diagnosis say to me that they don't feel like they experience the typical BPD traits. 'Classic BPD' express outwardly meaning they tend to lash out, speak their opinions and are quick to dispute anything they don't like. 'Quiet BPD' however is the opposite. People with 'Quiet BPD' tend to direct the same emotional responses inwardly, meaning, that they internalise negativity and hidden self-harm. This can push people with 'Quiet BPD' to engage in hidden self-harming or harmful behaviours because they are not getting the same emotional outlet as someone with 'Classic BPD'. That's not to say that someone with 'Classic BPD isn't likely to self-harm, it just means that someone with 'Quiet BPD' has more of a tendency to secretly and perhaps more intensely do so because they are so desperately trying to control the emotional storm inside.

'Classic BPD'

Please note that 'Classic BPD' is not and official category. People who experience 'Classic BPD' are said to externalise their emotions and express outwardly. This can mean that they might scream and shout a lot, cry a lot, get into physical or verbal fights or be promiscuous and often perceived as 'over dramatic'. This can lead to people assuming that someone with 'Classic BPD' traits are high maintenance, needy or attention seeking. 'Classic BPD' can present as extreme emotional outbursts that seem entirely real and valid to the person experiencing them. This may be down to the person being brought in an environment where anger has been openly expressed and acted upon.

'Quiet BPD'

Again, 'Quiet BPD' is not an official terminology but many with BPD can refer to how a 'Quiet BPD' struggle with expressing their emotions and instead internalising them. This could be down to their environmental upbringing where emotional outbursts were discouraged and/or conflict was usually avoided. Due to not feeling like they can express their emotions or that their emotions are invalid, people with 'Quiet BPD' are more likely to suppress their emotions. They can also mask their real emotions a lot, for instance they can give the illusion that they are fine, when actually they are not. It's not uncommon for a person with 'Quiet BPD' to want to please the people around them and they will do this even it they are uncomfortable or unhappy about it. For example, they may not feel like they can always say no to a person even when they want to. Additionally, they may go through phases of being completely open or completely shutting down.

How do I experience BPD?

BPD for me personally has been a learning curve as I've researched about the different unofficial types. I found myself wondering, well, which one am I? I mostly express inwardly and because of anxiety I am not one to shout and scream, however, I have issues with my anger. When I get angry, I see red, very quickly, and I lash out. I do currently have reins on my anger issues, but I still feel ready to explode when it hits. I have to really force myself to direct my anger outwardly in a safe space instead of inwardly and talk myself back down to a calm state. So, in consideration of all this, I would say I'm mostly fitting into the 'Quiet BPD' categorisation, however, sometimes I experience 'Classic BPD' traits. This is interesting because it you're wondering which one you are, you might also be 'a bit of both'!

Taking into consideration that you only need to be presenting with 5 of the BPD criteria to be diagnosed with BPD, you won't always match up to the exact specifics of the diagnosis. It may interest you to know that there are 256 possible combinations in which BPD can present. On top of this, it's important to note that even people presenting with the same match of BPD criteria will still considerably differ in how they experience BPD. Which raises the question of exactly how broad is the diagnoses of BPD? It comes down to the fact that your BPD diagnosis is unique to you. Just like with anything, people can experience similar things in their life, but they will never experience something 100% the exact same as the other person. Indeed, BPD can be a complex diagnosis to get to grips with. Your personal experience of BPD can be influenced by your individual personality, upbringing and if you have a comorbid diagnosis. So, if you find yourself questioning, 'what type of BPD do I experience?' or 'Why doesn't my BPD match with the typical traits?', It's simply the case that there is no universal cut and dry answer. People with BPD do not all behave in the same way. Our BPD is unique to us. See this as a good thing, it helps you to break away from the label of BPD and simply enhance the fact that you are you, no label needed.

What is comorbidity?

Comorbidity diagnosis means that you present with two diagnoses, disorders, or conditions at the same time. For instance, I am diagnosed with 'Generalised Anxiety Disorder' and of course, BPD. Whilst I had my diagnosis of GAD before BPD, when diagnosed BPD I still carried my diagnosis of GAD. Therefore, I have two diagnosis that are presenting at the same time. Comorbid diagnosis can occur in many different combinations of more than one diagnosis. To name but a few, PTSD, Depression, Addictions, Panic Disorder or Social Anxiety Disorder can be diagnosed on top of a BPD diagnosis.

Are we born with BPD?

This is actually a really common question- are we born with BPD? It's also a really difficult question to answer as the answer isn't the same for everyone with BPD. If we think about BPD being unique to us as previously mentioned, there lies the common issue. Many in the field of research for mental health and the BPD area specifically, have all drawn relatively similar conclusions about whether BPD is biological and/or developed over time.

The common opinion amongst most, it that BPD is down to both genetics and the early environment we are brought up in. It's said that we are born with the vulnerability of BPD and how we experience our childhood, really goes on to shape who we are as an adult and determines whether these vulnerabilities are trigged within us.

In terms of my own experiences, my mental health letters and medical records only spoke of 'childhood trauma', emphasis on the word 'trauma' because before I was diagnosed BPD, that is all they would really relay to me. Meaning, when I asked and asked and asked what was wrong with me. I always got the same answer of, nothing, it's down to trauma. So, from this, even after I was diagnosed with BPD, I assumed that my BPD had developed from the 'trauma' of which didn't happen until my late teens. Assuming it still fell into childhood trauma, even if it was late! I wouldn't say that in my early childhood I really experienced any kind of 'trauma', so it really was my only answer at the time.

When I started to meet more and more people with a BPD diagnosis, they would talk about this 'early childhood trauma', like that was the answer, loud and clear. This made me readdress my own diagnosis and experiences. How was it that I hadn't experienced what it seemed like everyone else had? But yet, I still present with the same Borderline traits as an adult? Confused and questioning whether I'd even been diagnosed correctly, I did my research!

Coming to learn that there were actually genetic factors involved with BPD, I then considered the question, was I born with BPD? I remembered back to as early as I possibly could within my childhood, and I realised something significant. When I was around 4 years old, I would display extreme disruptive behaviours in school. My family couldn't understand it, nothing was going at home, I was loved, and I didn't behave anything like that at home. My parents even asked at the social clubs I attended, and they reported no behaviour issues or anything of concern. Some of my earliest memories include, climbing over stacked chairs whilst the rest of my class were having carpet time, getting shouted at and actually enjoying it and running out of class at any given opportunity. One week, the headteacher said to me, "If you can be good for one week, you will get something really special". In every class or activity, the teachers encouraged me to take part and gave me the extra attention that enabled me to 'be good'. Come the end of the week in assembly, the headteacher announced that they had a special award. When my name was called, I wondered up to the stage, the whole school clapping me, the feeling was something I'd never felt before. I was proud, and I felt validated and cared for. I loved the feeling, but soon after, the encouragement and attention was diverted away from me again, and very quickly, my behaviour returned.

Reflecting back on this time as an adult, I see that, for some reason, I desperately craved the love and attention. I see that I would split between loving the teachers when they validated me and hating them when they ignored me. That even as a 4-year-old, I would manipulate the teachers into giving me what I desired. On some level I knew what I was doing, I knew which behaviours were going to get which consequences, or which attention I hungered for and I knew that the moment I stopped would be the moment that I'd lose this. I'd also change my identity depending on which environment I was in, for example, being happy at social clubs, content at home or badly behaved at school. I'd get angry if I felt unheard, I'd feel empty because no one wanted to be friends with the 'naughty girl' and I'd feel rejected and paranoid about opinions. For a 4-year-old, this is a lot and it also shows that even a as 4-year-old I was showing signs of BPD. It was there, all along, it was there…

In conclusion, I do believe that I was born with BPD, certain triggers at different stages of my life set off the vulnerabilities I already had inside. Which in turn, also made me vulnerable to experiencing the 'traumas' that I did in my teens.

BPD can be developed overtime without genetic

factors, due to trauma alone, although this seems to be seen as a rarity. So, for the most part, according to latest research, we are born the underlying concept of BPD, it is whether we are triggering are vulnerabilities in early childhood that really determine whether we will be diagnosed with BPD in later life.

I hope this has been informative for you, unfortunately, there is no clear cut and dry answer to the question. If you look over your past, as did I, you may come to find the answer for yourself.

My personal experience and how it has inspired me to help others.

In my personal experience of being diagnosed, having already done my research beforehand, when my psychologist told me I was being diagnosed with BPD, he asked me if I'd heard of it, to which I replied, yes. I don't know if he assumed because I'd heard of it that he didn't need to explain, but I was given no explanation or support plan. When I returned a few months later, I asked if it was possible to be put forward for DBT (Dialectical behaviour therapy), to which, and I quote, he replied; "DBT is only available for those who self-harm on a massive scale." The answer was neither helpful nor it inspire me to stop self-harming at the time. I was absolutely outraged that he has given me this answer. I did not increase my levels of self-harm, but I was aware that some others may have done in order the get the help. Since this day (nearly 5 years ago) I have been on a journey to try and find answers, support and ways to cope with the diagnosis. I have researched and collectively put into practice anything that might help. I have had to make many changes and adaptions to the resources I have found, but over time have developed methods that work for me. I needed to get to a position where I fully understood BPD and how best to go about **taking back control** of my life, as well as, maintaining the practice of this. Five years on and I'm ready to share this in the hope that it may help others in the same position.

Recognising BPD emotions

The following nine points are the criteria for diagnosis of BPD explained in further detail:

Frantic efforts to avoid real or imagined abandonment.

People with BPD often live in a constant state of fear of abandonment. They fear they will be abandoned and as a result make frantic efforts, real or imagined, to prevent this from happening.

This fear of impending separation, rejection or the loss of external structures can lead to profound changes in behaviour, self-image, mood/emotions and thoughts.

For some of us with BPD, we build barriers around ourselves and shut people out, so we don't have to deal with people getting too close and them abandoning us. Others may do the opposite, and frantically make efforts to keep people close by always trying to keep them happy.

The fear of abandonment for someone with BPD is very real. They may only have temporary separation from someone but can feel intense fears as a result. Changes to plans my also cause the onset of fears.

Taking Back Control- BPD

These fears may manifest themselves as:

- Jealous fits of rage

- Emotional withdrawal

- Damaging relationships

- Impulsive actions

- Lashing out with words

Image curtesy of Vicky Vaughan

A pattern of unstable or intense interpersonal relationships categorised by alternating between extremes of idealisation and devaluation.

People with BPD often experience a pattern of unstable or intense interpersonal relationships, finding themselves fluctuating from one emotion to another. For some us we find that we 'SPLIT' between extremely loving a person or extremely hating them. This can be very confusing as we don't always know how we feel about a person from one day to the next. We are constantly in a cycle of idealising others or devaluing them. In other words, positive and negative attributes of a person are not joined together into a cohesive set of beliefs. We may also 'SPLIT' over the way we feel about and for ourselves or over how we think others feel for us. You can read more about 'splitting' in the next section of this chapter. While strongly desiring intimacy, people with BPD tend towards disorderly attachment patterns in relationships: insecure, avoidant or ambivalent attachment patterns and fearfully preoccupied attachment patterns are not uncommon in relationships. Image curtesy of Vicky Vaughan

Identity disturbance: Markedly and persistently unstable self-image or sense of self.

People with BPD struggle with identity, self-image or sense of sense. Simply feeling like they are 'non-existent', or they feel like a chameleon changing who they are depending on circumstances and what they think others want from them.

Changing due to situation and environment is something everyone does to some degree, however with BPD it is more markedly recognisable. Thoughts and feelings can also change to match current behaviours. In addition to this, People with BPD can struggle with determining where their identity ends and where the identity of others begins. Subsequently, this makes it difficult to sometimes know where healthy personal boundaries lie. For some of us, it's hard to pinpoint our own identity when it's constantly changing and therefore, we can find ourselves mirroring other people's identities

Image curtesy of Vicky Vaughan

Impulsivity in at least two areas that are potentially self-damaging.

Impulsivity is often an emotional response to something negative that has happened. It can lead us to act quickly, without thinking of the consequences to our actions. Understandably but sadly having detrimental effects on our relationships, physical health and finances. Not to mention the legal implications for some impulsivities.

People with BPD can act impulsively to try and get some sort of immediate antidote to their emotional pain, but this antidote is short lived and we tend to feel shame or guilt afterwards for the actions that we have carried out. We can find ourselves trapped in a worsening cycle with this. Feel emotional pain- Engage in impulsive behaviours to relieve that pain- Feel shame and guilt over the actions- Feel emotional pain from shame and guilt- Feel stronger urges to engage in impulsive behaviours to relieve pain.

Image curtesy of Vicky Vaughan

Recurrent suicidal behaviour, gestures, or threats, or self-mutilating behaviour.

People with BPD can experience recurrent suicidal behaviour, gestures, or threats, or self-mutilating behaviour. This might occur for a number of different reasons, such as, expressing anger, self-punishment, generating normal feelings, taking away the feelings or distracting from difficult circumstances and emotional pain.

This behaviour is usually a response to emotional pain or trauma. Additionally, it is also not uncommon for trichotillomania and eating disorders to be considered as a form of self-harm. These are often diagnosed as comorbid conditions in people with BPD.

Image curtesy of Vicky Vaughan

Affective instability due to a marked reactivity of mood.

This often means that people with BPD are affected by intense episodic dysphoria, irritability, or anxiety. We experience rapid mood swings that are more intense than a neurotypical person. Our extreme mood swings change from one end of the scale to the other in a matter of seconds. Due to the experience of being on this emotional roller coaster, it isn't uncommon for those with BPD to feel overwhelmed and emotionally exhausted by it all.

BPD is often confused with Bipolar Disorder because of the similarity between symptoms (mood swings and impulsivity). The difference between them, is that BPD mood swings happen more rapidly and are more frequent, BPD mood swings are more specific and are more dependent on the positives and negatives for what's going on.

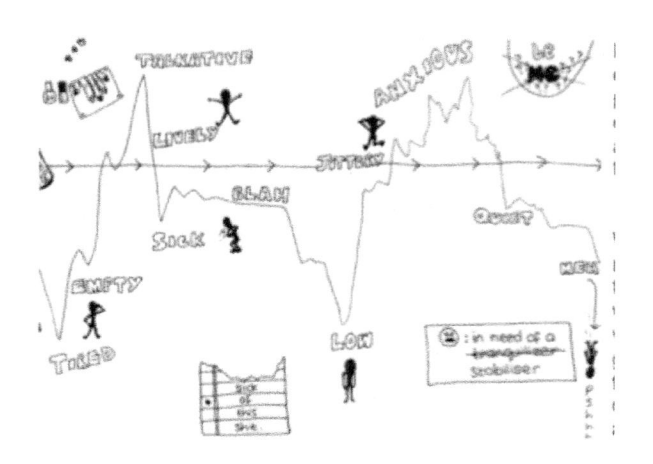

Image curtesy of Vicky Vaughan

Chronic feelings of emptiness.

Many people find that they have choric feelings of emptiness with BPD. As well as intense feelings of loneliness they may experience extreme feelings of boredom like there is a void that needs to be filled. Some say it's like a sensation in their abdomen or chest of an empty hole that can't be filled or that they feel restless.

Chronic feelings of emptiness are also often linked to the way one feels about career plans, personal ideals, opinions, attitudes, lifestyle and sexual orientation to name a few. These feelings may arise from 'not feeling good enough' or the conflicting sense of self like previously mentioned.

Many with BPD will try various different things in an effort to try to fill the empty void, which unfortunately, often means turning to unhealthy impulsions or self-injury. Often resulting panic attacks and self-loathing.

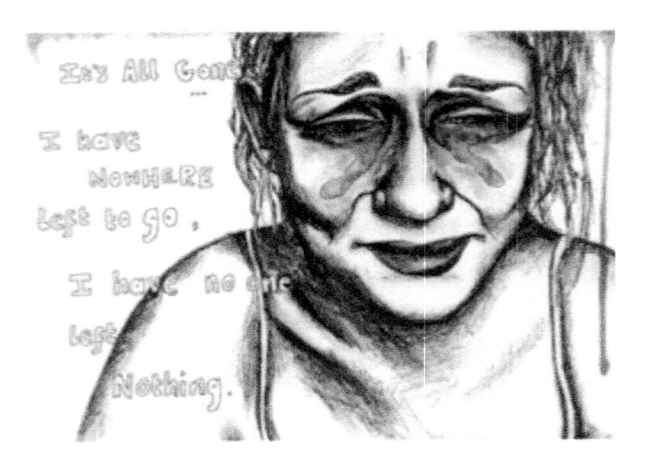

Image curtesy of Vicky Vaughan

Inappropriate, intense anger or difficulty controlling anger.

These intense emotions of rage are sometimes described as 'borderline rage' and can be so compelling for someone with BPD. Compelling in the sense that they change the behaviour of the person experiencing it in a matter of seconds. It's not uncommon to hear that someone with BPD has uncontrollable rage. This can include frequent displays of temper, constant anger, throwing or breaking things or physical fights.

To a neurotypical person, BPD anger may seem over the top or inappropriate. People with BPD experience anger for reasons that others may see as 'no big deal', however, it is very real for a person with BPD. Many people with BPD fear the anger because of its intensities. They would rather keep their anger unseen and avoid letting it out at all costs. As a result, they internalise the anger, they may dissociate with it or experience derealisation and/or depersonalisation. Derealisation is where a person feels the world around them isn't real. Depersonalisation is where a person doesn't feel like they are real. They can often occur at the same time.

Image curtesy of Vicky Vaughan

Transient, stress-related paranoid ideation or severe dissociative symptoms.

Transient, stress related paranoid ideation or severe dissociative symptoms is similarly comparable (in some cases) to psychotic-like symptoms. People with BPD may experience things including (but not limited to) paranoid feelings through misinterpretation of real-life events, delusions that people are harming or abandoning them, hallucinations which result in not knowing what's real and what isn't, and depersonalisation.

Unlike delusional psychosis experienced by those with psychotic disorders, people with BPD usually experience these psychotic episodes on a short-term basis. They do however experience the symptoms of delusional psychosis with the same intensity as those with delusional disorders.

Additionally, people with BPD can often feel detached from their thoughts, feelings and real life. Many say it can be like being on extreme autopilot or feeling numb and disconnected from their physical bodies. In extreme cases this can lead to being unable to recall chunks of time or a complete block of memories.

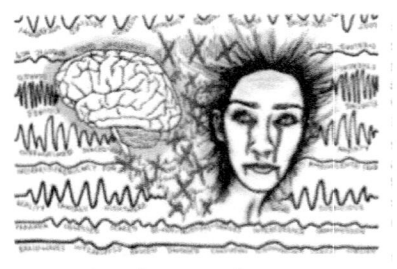

Image curtesy of Vicky Vaughan

And breathe.... Because that was a lot of intense and overwhelming information to take in. Take a moment here to give yourself some space to breath and a moments rest.

The Japanese symbol for peace

Part 2: Managing BPD Emotions
Splitting

Splitting is a term which is used to describe how one splits their emotional state to either extremes of a high mood or a low mood. These are often described as "black" and "white" with no in between. There are different ways in which you can experience splitting.

- People splitting- People splitting refers to how we feel about another person. When a person does something that we dislike, in that moment we hate them, however, when a person does something we like, in that moment we love them. We either extremely love them or extremely hate them and this can change in a matter of seconds. On the flip side, we can also split between thinking someone loves or hates us. This is usually more prevalent in 'quiet borderlines'.

- Situational splitting- Situation splitting refers to how we feel about a situation. When something is going our way then we feel all good but when something is going wrong then we feel all bad. These good and bad emotions are extreme to the point where we either feel like it's the best thing in the world or the worse thing in the world.

- Mood splitting- Mood splitting is sometimes without cause or an internal trigger and refers to the way in which we feel in ourselves. Again, just like the previous splitting, this can be one extreme to the other in a matter of seconds and can often cause dissociation and depersonalisation.

I have used black and white splitting as the inspiration behind the book cover. Along with the bright colours to represent that we need not only feel in black and white. BPD can often lead us to believe we can only feel in "black" and "white", but I believe different. I believe we are able to experience emotions in all colours.

We feel in colour!

How do we feel in colour?

Instead of splitting black and white, we must learn to find ourselves in the middle somewhere. How we do that is to consciously think of alternative ways of describing what we feel. For example, if you split between loving and hating someone we can change this to something like; *I dislike the way you are behaving right now, it's causing me hurt and upset, I find this frustrating but I still love you.*

There is room to feel all of these things instead of limiting yourself to one emotion at different ends of the scale. If something is 'all good' or 'all bad' we must remind ourselves to weight up an equal perspective for the situation. For instance, if you split between 'all good' and 'all bad' about having to work from home, (which is common at the time of writing this book because of the Covid-19 pandemic) we can change this to something like; *I enjoy working from because I can focus more but sometimes I feel frustrated that I don't have all the resources I would usually have at the office.*

We can feel both of these things in the same moment and have an equal perspective of our feelings, so we are not pushed back and forth from 'all good' or 'all bad'.

Idealisation vs devaluing (push & pull)

Having BPD can mean that we see people as 'always good' or 'always bad'. When they do something to upset us, we 'push' them away and truly believe that this person is 'always bad'. When they do something we like, we 'pull' them back and again, truly believe that they are 'always good'. It's a confusing and vicious cycle to be constantly stuck in and can end up driving the person away when they grow tired of our push and pull affects. Which subsequently, only re-confirms our belief that people will abandon us.

Again, we must learn to find middle ground with this. We must remind ourselves that everyone has good attributes and bad attributes and the real key point here is... they have these at the same time! Let me be clear here, and say that, when I used the term 'bad' it doesn't mean that a person is 'bad. It is just representational of the splitting scale of either 'always good' or 'always bad', demonstrating extremes at both ends. It requires us to use alternatives such as; *I really enjoy this persons company but I dislike that they can sometimes be unsensitive about things*, or, *I feel really disheartened by their behaviour today but I don't dislike them because of it.*

It has come to my attention that some people with BPD experience what is known in the BPD community as 'Giving or retracting splitting'. Meaning, that they split between extremely giving and extremely retracting'. I unfortunately don't have much personal experience when it comes to this, however, I do have a suggestion that make be of use if you do experience this.

Taking Back Control- BPD

When you find yourself spitting from one end of the scale to the other, practice focusing on a middle boundary level. What I mean by this, similar to the previous splitting concepts with finding the middle ground, is you must also find some middle ground. You don't have to fall directly on-top of the boundary level but fall as close as you possibly can to it.

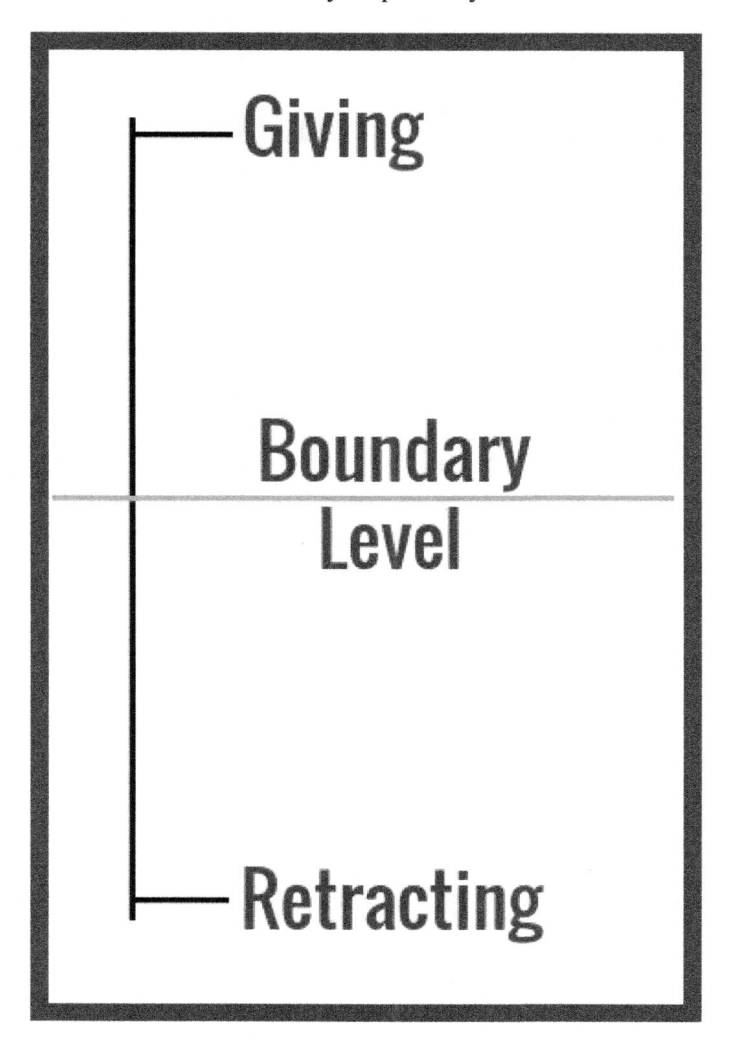

Giving

Boundary Level

Retracting

For instance, if you're the type of person who is 'all giving', then you give in general, or you give a lot of yourself to others. You're also likely to be the type of person who retracts back into themselves, which others may perceive as you pushing them away, and ultimately, you feel like they don't care. To bring yourself away from the extremes of this negative splitting, set your own boundaries, give a little but equally give yourself a little space when needed. The idea of the boundary level isn't to fall directly on the line, it is to fall as close as possible to either side. If you feel you want to give, then give a little, but don't stray too far up the scale from the boundary level. If you feel like retracting, then give yourself that little bit of time and space, but don't stray too far down the scale from the boundary level. The idea is that it gives you the opportunity to experience both within reason without compromise to your mental health.

Important takeaways:

1. **Remember to take the time to find middle ground or fall close to the boundary level.**

2. **Choose alternative ways to describe your feelings.**

3. **Weigh up an equal perspective.**

4. **People have both 'good' and 'bad' things about them at the same time.**

5. **We have room to feel all different types of emotions, all at once.**

We feel in colour!

Favourite person

Favorite person is a term used within the BPD community, although not many people are aware of it. I thought I would shed some light on the matter given that I have had past favourite persons bordering on obsessions. I have had my share of bad experiences relating to these and they have been challenging to overcome.

So, what is a favorite person?

A favourite person can be anyone that you feel compelled to connect with. You idolise them and you find yourself desperate for their acceptance. They can make you feel like you live for them instead of you living for yourself. A favourite person is more than a best friend. They are someone who you focus your entire efforts on, and you need to know everything about them, where and what they are doing. You may also feel like you need to change your own opinions and values to match up to theirs. You feel the need to be close to your favourite person, all of the time and you feel lost when they are not there. They provide a sense of security, comfort and loving attention that you so desperately crave and often we end up falling, deeply and quickly in love with these people.

A favourite person can be a loved one, a friend, someone who you've just met and even someone who you haven't met. A favourite person can be anyone. You can feel incredible intense emotions towards them. You will do anything to keep you favourite person close through fear of losing them and you may get jealous when they see other people instead of you. You feel like you need them to define you and you don't know how you could ever live without them.

Is having a favourite person a bad thing?

It doesn't have to be, although I issue a word of warning with this because having a healthy favourite person relationship is possible, but it can also very hard to maintain.

One of the most common problems with having a favourite person is that in trying to seek the attachment to them you end up pushing them away. We have a tendency to act impulsively around them and, in some ways, (not always knowingly) manipulate them into reciprocating the feelings. A common BPD response is the push and pull effect. We can often mis-lead our favourite person into having a somewhat fabricated disagreement (push) so that we can make up and have them apologising and momentarily receiving their full attention and love (pull). Subsequently, in the long run, this will drive your favourite person away for good and our fears of abandonment become reinforced.

Recognising that your favourite person relationship is starting to become toxic is important but frustratingly challenging. I have had three favourite people in my past. Each time the intensity of these compelling emotions got stronger. These all ended with the other person pulling away for one reason or another. The toxicity of my third favourite person relationship threw me into an unhealthy state of obsession and verged dangerously into stalking.

In my own experiences of dealing with favourite person, I placed my people so high on a pedestal and felt they could do no wrong. This meant that my expectations of the relationships were impossible to be met by the people involved. No one is perfect and yet you feel like your favourite person gives you the illusion that they are perfection. It's like being sucked into a vortex where only you and the other person exists and while this can be a comforting delusion it isn't realistic and can be extremely damaging to your mental and physical wellbeing. It can lead you to unpredictable behaviours and a total loss of control over your own actions. This can also cross over into splitting in the sense that if your favourite person is giving you your desired attachment then they are loved whole-heartedly by you. However, when they don't meet your expectations, say something that diminishes the connection or start to distance from you, they become hated. There is no in-between and you can be stuck in a loop of a love-hate relationship where you go from idolising them to devaluing them.

Fear not.... although this is deep, intense and can be extremely overwhelming, your favourite person relationships do not have be like this. You can create a healthy favourite person relationship if you manage it correctly.

How to have a healthy favourite person relationship.

- First and foremost, recognising the early signs of favourite person is important.

- Attraction
- A craving for acceptance
- Thinking about them constantly
- Wanting to be with them all the time
- A feeling of fear when they don't contact you
- Splitting, love-hate, idolising -devaluing
- Jealousy
- Fear of rejection
- Fear of abandonment

You may not experience all of these and you may experience more. It is different for different people. In my experience, it happens hard and fast and feels something entirely on a whole new level to a best friend relationship. I never really knew much about favourite person, so I just thought this was what feeling in love felt like. I never felt like that for my partner at the time even though I did love her. This was confusing for me but when I had heard about favourite person and had done my research, I knew without question, that I had been experiencing favourite person.

- Be YOU not them

It's important to know who you are. Think about your values and your beliefs. Think about your identity. You need to gain some self-understanding so that you are not letting yourself become defined by your favourite person. This can be difficult if you find yourself mirroring your favourite persons values, beliefs, opinions and identity. Take some time to really think about who you were before but also take the time to think about who YOU want to be right now. Having a favourite person can change you, so much so that you may lose your old identity entirely. This is okay, we as humans are always, growing, learning and changing throughout our lives. We can shape new identities. After my third favourite person, I'd lost myself so much that I gave up finding my original self and created a new identity. Do you remember in chapter 2 where I mentioned the song- Supposed to be? This was the transitional period I was referring to. It can take time to re-shape your Identity, just remember to always stay true to yourself and be allowing of the process. It is scary but it really does pay off. You could look back over chapter 1 if you feel you need some extra support with this.

- Challenge your thoughts

Everything is telling you that your favourite person is the ultimate creation of perfection. Challenge these thoughts, remind yourself that they are just a regular person at the end of the day. Challenge your negative thoughts that are telling you that you need this person, that this person defines you and that you can't live without them. You do not need your favourite person to define you or validate your self-worth.

-Evaluate the relationship

You need to weigh up whether you are going to continue a relationship between you and your favourite person or not.*

You need to ask yourself these questions:

- What does my favourite person bring to this relationship?
- How do they make me feel?
- What am I getting out of this relationship?
- Can I continue this relationship without a negative impact to my mental wellbeing?

These questions are difficult, so don't feel too pressured to answer them straight away. You may want to allow time and think about these over a period where you are continuing the relationship to help you pinpoint your answers. It's also important to allow yourself past the reluctance and denial that these questions might trigger. Whilst it is easy to want to ignore these questions, you must accept that these are crucial and learn to put yourself first.

*Please only do this if you're in a safe position to do so, if you feel you aren't, don't change anything until you speak with a professional counselor or therapist.

- Be open and honest

In my experience it's a good idea to be open and honest with your favourite person about how you feel towards them and make sure they are aware that you may need extra reassurance about the security of your relationship. If your favourite person is understanding of this, you are in a better position to maintain the relationship going forward. If for whatever reason they are not, it is so important, however hard this may seem, to discontinue the relationship. Trying to move forward would only fuel your need for acceptance, self-worth and attachment and eventually lead into the toxic relationship that you need to avoid.

- Rationalise

Maintaining a healthy favourite person relationship requires you to be rational. We need to try and control the cycle of the love-hate relationship. How we do this is to rationalise. Instead of having your tunnel vision of knocking your favourite person off the pedestal every time they upset you, we need to not place them on the pedestal to begin with.

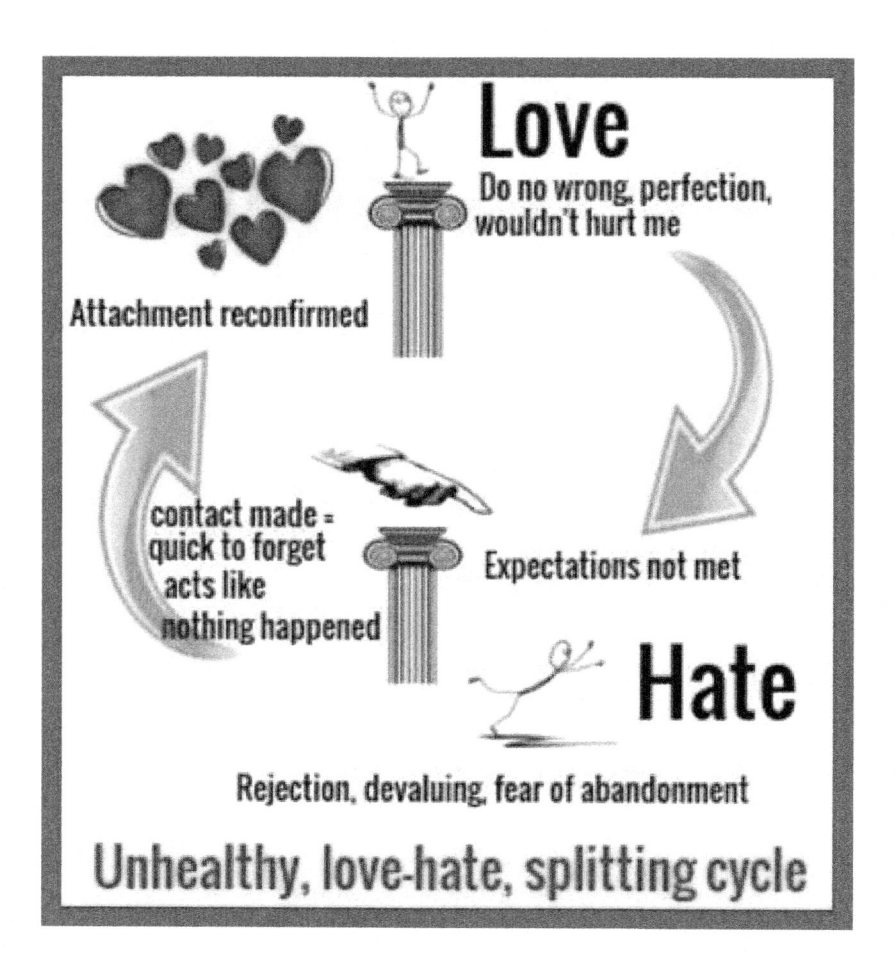

Love — Do no wrong, perfection, wouldn't hurt me

Attachment reconfirmed

contact made = quick to forget acts like nothing happened

Expectations not met

Hate

Rejection, devaluing, fear of abandonment

Unhealthy, love-hate, splitting cycle

Taking Back Control - BPD

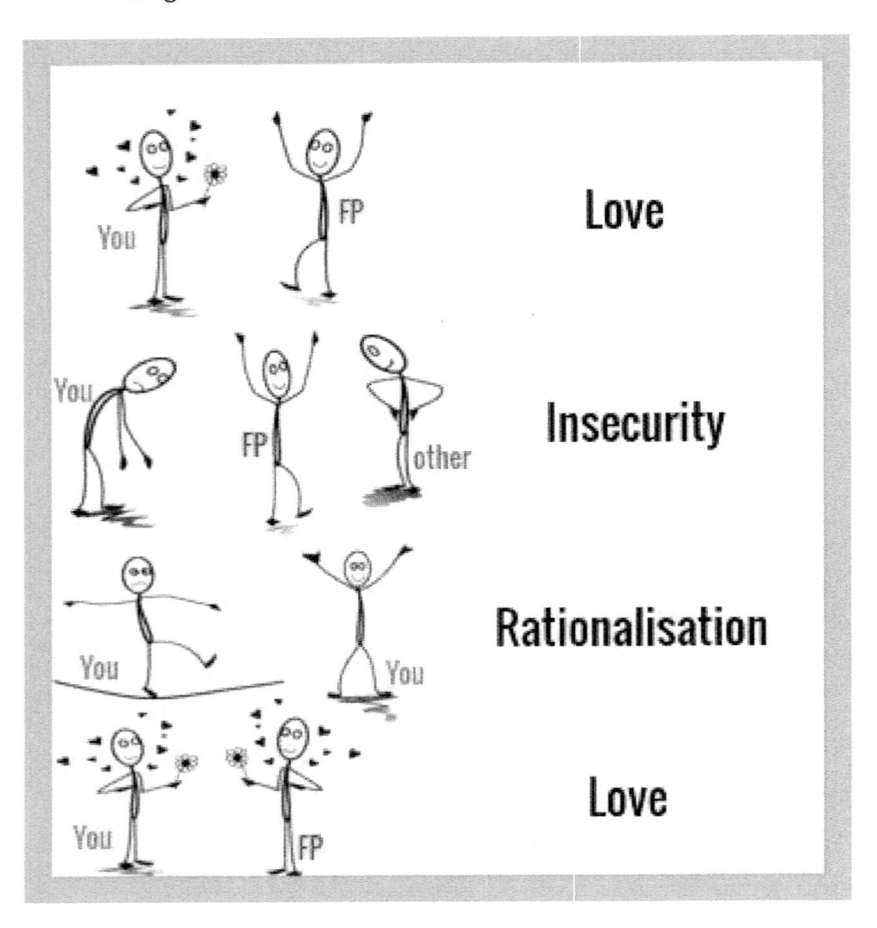

Love

Insecurity

Rationalisation

Love

You need to remember that your favourite person is human and will make mistakes. You need to remember that they are allowed to see and have other friends outside of you. You need to respect that sometimes they may want their space just as equally as you may want your own from time to time. Rationalisation gives you the acceptance and permission to view the situation from a different perspective. If your favourite person loves and cares for you then they will return, and you won't be trapped in the love-hate relationship which is only going to drive your favourite person away in the end.

What other things could be useful?

- Build yourself a support network so you can have support around you should you ever feel like you need something that your favourite person isn't giving you. For instance, the reassurance that you are loved and worthy.
- Practice self-love and build a positive self-image.
- Have friends outside your favourite person relationship.
- Get a hobby- distraction helps!
- Build a self-care package for when you have to rationalise. (refer to self-care chapter and the coping techniques for help with this)
- Express the intense emotions through creative expressive arts.
- **Always seek professional or medical help if you are struggling to maintain control over your favourite person emotions and behaviours.**

I hope that this has helped you to gain more of an understanding of favourite person. Having a favourite person doesn't have to be a bad thing. Do your best to maintain a healthy favourite person relationship and they can be something uniquely special.

BPD Anger

BPD Anger is one of the main criteria of the BPD diagnosis. Anger in itself is actually a healthy emotion to have, everyone experiences anger. It is however more frequent and intensified for someone with BPD. As if the anger in itself isn't enough challenge, we then have the challenge of trying to control it and our behaviours. 'Borderline rage' is often the term recognised in the BPD community which is also commonly paired with 'uncontrollable rage'. Uncontrollable rage means that we lose all control over our behaviour during an episode of anger.

Having BPD means that we feel the anger to the extreme. We fear our loss of control and our behaviours as a consequence. In an effort to try to and keep it hidden, we can often suppress this anger, but the problem is, the anger is still there. We fight against ourselves for as long as we can until the anger overflows, and we end up exploding our unwanted anger in full force.

I recently had a conversation with a friend of whom had been experiencing unwanted anger due to some difficulties with her child. My friend has a BPD diagnosis, and she suspects her child may have ASD. So, you can see why she came to me for advice! She had previously spoken to another friend who had said to her- Emma doesn't get angry about the situation, so why are you? Which ultimately made my friend in question feel like she wasn't allowed to feel this way and gave her the message that she was a bad parent. My response was- In some way I'm glad I give people that illusion, but it is far from the truth! I get angry, I get anger more times than I wish to mention. ASD in a young child is an extremely challenging thing, add on top of that a BPD diagnosis and it sends things into overdrive. I've never felt like BPD and ASD are a good mix. A lot of the behaviours that my son presents with, send me into a constant state of frustration. One being that he is so fussy about his food, I will carefully select and prepare him a meal, then he will throw his plate across the room and go into meltdown about it. It's a frustrating situation for anyone to be in let alone someone with BPD. There have been many occasions where I've left my son to cry, because I needed to cry too and there was still spaghetti Bolognese splattered up the walls and furniture. Another thing that really angers me is his constant state of hyperactivity. Whilst I'm constantly trying to keep my mentality calm and positive, he comes in a like a tornado and it sets me on edge. I literally find myself saying a hundred times a day- Can we just have some calm now? Because I need the breathing space, otherwise things build up and lead to an angry outburst, then I shut down.

My point being in all of this, is that yes, I DO get angry, but that doesn't make me a bad parent. I always remember the most important thing in every 'borderline rage' situation, which is to keep everyone safe. Undoubtedly, that anger and frustration needs to come out, it just has to! I always make sure my son is in a safe place, then I walk away, breath.... Take a moment and then return to the situation. There are times when I can't do this, and the angry spills out vocally, and then I often feel guilty about raising my voice almost instantly, however, it still doesn't make me a bad parent. I realise that straight away that I'm expressing my anger towards my son, I then place him on the thinking step. The thinking step is just as much for my benefit as it is also for Finley's. I don't believe in the word punishment because Finley doesn't always mean to be 'naughty' or do so knowingly. So, we have the thinking step, Finley will stay sitting on the step for a couple of minutes. Then I can use that time to take myself away and directly express my anger elsewhere and in a safe space. Then I return to Finley, I sign, I'm sorry. I don't ask him to say sign it back, but he often does. We cuddle and then carry on with our day. I'm no mum of year, but I'm learning to not shut my anger out, feel it, express it safely, and then continue feeling much better.

I know that everyone won't agree with my parenting style and it's fine for people to have their opinion on it, but I just wanted to explain to my friend that It's fine to get angry, it's normal. It's about how to you direct that anger that's important. Every parent gets angry with their children, they do, but it doesn't make them a bad parent. You don't have to apply this to just parenting, it can work for yourself too. Getting angry about a situation, doesn't make you a bad person, it makes you a 'normal' person. In summary, releasing anger is healthy, choosing how to do so in the right way is paramount.

Fight or flight is our usual response. We have an adrenaline build up, this can increase your heart rate, you may sweat or shake, and you feel the uncontrollable urge to either fight or flight. Here are some useful suggestions for fight and flight responses that are safe:

- Scream into a pillow
- Punch a pillow
- Scribble on a piece of paper
- Free writing
- Clench your fists and scream
- Kick or bounce a ball in the garden
- Do some push-ups
- Run on the spot
- Break material, plastic bag, paper, cardboard.
- Vent, talk to yourself out loud
- Squeeze playdough
- Smash ice in the bath
- Build a tower, knock it down
- Sing or dance away your anger
- Make a cake, smash it
- Pop balloons
- Scrub your bathroom
- Spin something

Useful self-help suggestions for managing BPD Emotions

Letter to self
Writing a letter to yourself may sound silly but it really gets you thinking about positives you can say to yourself. You can refer back to your letter when you need a little self-encouragement. Another nice idea is to ask a friend to post the letter back to you at a later date. If you don't know when your friend is going to post it, then it's a nice thing to pick up and read when your mail arrives. You can also do what I 'accidentally' did and leave the letter in a notebook and forget about it. I dug out all my old notebooks and brushed the dust off them to help me write this book and I came across a Letter to self I did 4 years ago! What I loved about reading it back is that I'd written things that I can now look back on and say, I got through them struggles! It brought tears to my eyes and filled my heart with such immense pride for myself.

There are going to be hard times ahead but need to find coping strategies that work for you and practice them every day. I know you feel like you've lost all your safety nets and it's left you feeling lost, but you will adjust, you have already started and you're doing an amazing job. Remember, the more overthinking, the harder it is, just go for it, it's working so far. Always remember to be yourself, the real you. Stick with it, it will get easier and it will be worth it.

Writing

Of course I like writing, I've written a book! Over the years I've collected many notebooks and filled them with just about everything, poems, stories, song lyrics, useful information from research, ideas, letters, scribble. I honestly could go on and on, but I won't! The point I'm trying to make here is that it has helped in in various ways such as being able to express myself, serve as a constant reminder to engage in self-help, to heal and to compartmentalise my life. What I mean by compartmentalise is that there has been a different notebook for each section of my journey to date. For example, one of my notebooks is purely letters to my old therapist from years ago. When I left therapy, I felt like I wasn't ready and one of the things I did to cope was to write a letter every week to my old therapist. I never sent the letters, but in writing down what I would had said if I was actually in a therapy session, it helped me to feel like I'd released what I'd needed to. I did this for about a year!

Here are a couple of extracts from my letters:

- *I retreat, I retreat from everything. It's pains me so much. I feel butterflies and these butterflies are bruising. No matter how hard I try and block it all, it's always there.*

- *I think I have Borderline Personality Disorder, it all links and makes sense. I'd feel less crazy with this disorder because I'd understand why I can't think/feel like other people do. It would set me apart from being normal but yet I'd feel more normal with it. I'm hanging on in there.*

- *It's a year on and who'd of thought I'd still be writing these darn things! It helps me, I'm happy to keep the crazy in this book and close it, put it back on the shelf and walk away. It's all I have right now.*

Eating Disorders

I don't have much experience or knowledge when it comes to eating disorders. I have however had difficulties regarding my eating patterns, although I've never been diagnosed with having an eating disorder, I have experienced spouts of unhealthy eating patterns lasting serval months at a time. I've always struggled with being overweight so in these phases I didn't give myself permission to eat unless I felt like I deserved to, it was essentially a form of punishment. My poor pattern of eating phases have now subsided, but I do find myself slipping back there from time to time. To stop myself, I set reminders on my phone to eat, I find that eating little and often works better for me and I also ensure that I am eating healthily and taking part in one form of exercise per day. I still feel the same, but I am dealing with it in a healthy alternative way.

Sarah Eley, the founder of Borderline Arts has written a useful article on the link between BPD and Eating Disorders. You can read the article on the Borderline Arts website: www.borderlinearts.org
Go to the about us tab and click on articles.

Taking Back Control- BPD

Irrational thinking VS rational thinking

Feeling overwhelmed about a situation?

Try dividing your irrational and rational thoughts about the situation and use the rational thoughts to help you rationalise your way through it.

Irrational	Rational

Reflection & Evaluation

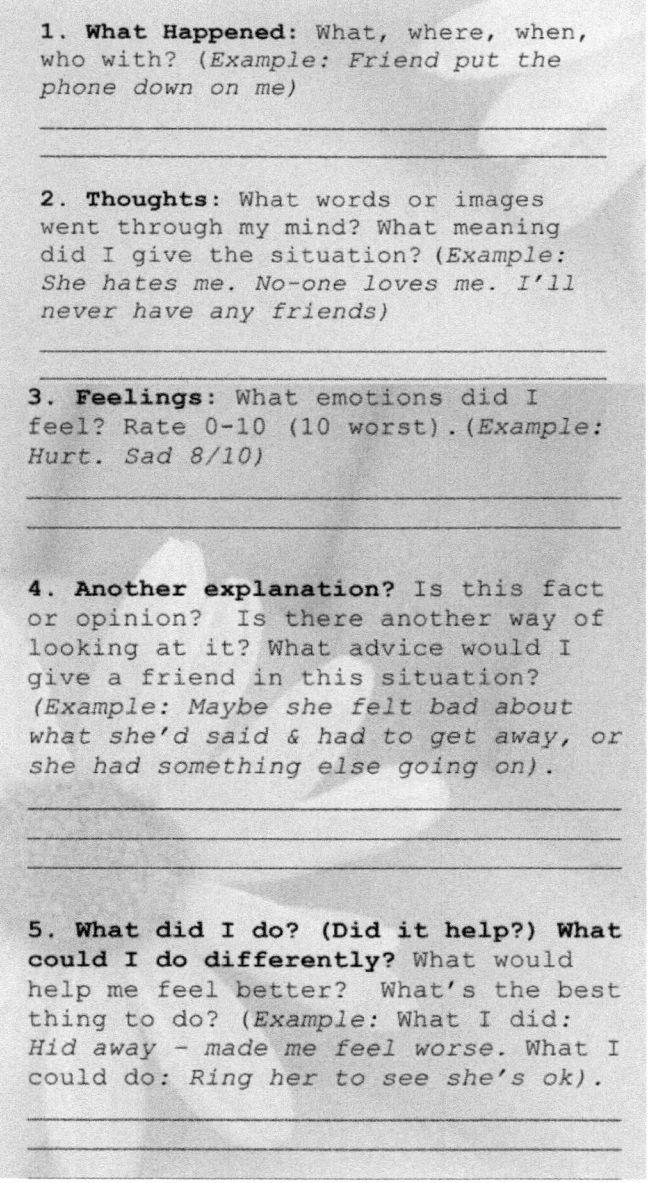

1. What Happened: What, where, when, who with? (*Example: Friend put the phone down on me*)
_____
_____

2. Thoughts: What words or images went through my mind? What meaning did I give the situation? (*Example: She hates me. No-one loves me. I'll never have any friends*)
_____

3. Feelings: What emotions did I feel? Rate 0-10 (10 worst). (*Example: Hurt. Sad 8/10*)
_____
_____

4. Another explanation? Is this fact or opinion? Is there another way of looking at it? What advice would I give a friend in this situation? (*Example: Maybe she felt bad about what she'd said & had to get away, or she had something else going on*).
_____
_____

5. What did I do? (Did it help?) What could I do differently? What would help me feel better? What's the best thing to do? (*Example: What I did: Hid away - made me feel worse. What I could do: Ring her to see she's ok*).
_____
_____

Image curtesy of Sarah Eley

Categorising through colours

Sometimes I find it helpful to refer to feeling things in colours, hence the reasoning behind the- we feel in colour motto. This is how I categorise my colours with how I associate my feelings with them. You may wish to categorise them differently as we can each interrupt colours differently.

Red- Anger. Aggression. Frustration.

Pale Blue- Calm. Trust. Stability.

Orange- Comfort. Security. Protection.

Purple- Wisdom. Creativity. Curiosity.

Yellow- Happy. Contentedness. Optimistic.

Black- Bitterness. Jealousy. Confliction. Loneliness.

White- Clarity. Wholeness. Cathartic. Euphoric. Bliss.

Green- Harmony. Balance. Growth. Strength. Courage.

Pink- Romantic. Passionate. Inspired. Love. Ambition.

It serves as another reminder, that I feel in colour.

Taking Back Control - BPD

Contract to self

Set your taking back control intentions by making a promise to yourself to be committed to your recovery. Sign and date it, then refer back to this whenever you need reminding in your own words why you're doing this.

```
Commitment to Recover           Congratulations!!!

Today I commit to tackle my     When I have made this commitment to
difficulty/illness that I call  myself, it sometimes feels a bit
_____   suffocating and scary. But I find
                                that it helps to remember that it
I acknowledge that this means   is MY decision. I always have
letting go of _____  permission to change my mind - but
_____   if I do find yourself thinking
                                about giving up, I try to make sure
                                I read through my reasons why I am
I realise that some days will go  doing what I am doing first, as
well and that some days I might sometimes I just need reminding to
feel like a disaster and I might reignite a sense of motivation and
feel like giving up, but I am   determination.
doing this because _____
_____   Another thing I find helps is to
_____   congratulate myself on making such
                                an often tough, positive decision
and as hard as it may be, this  and to give myself a little treat
is my commitment that I am      as a reward! This may be a lush
making to myself.               bath bomb, a special chocolate bar,
                                anything which makes me feel good
Signed _____ Date _____ (In a balanced/healthy/not breaking
                                the bank sort of way!)
```

Image curtesy of Sarah Eley

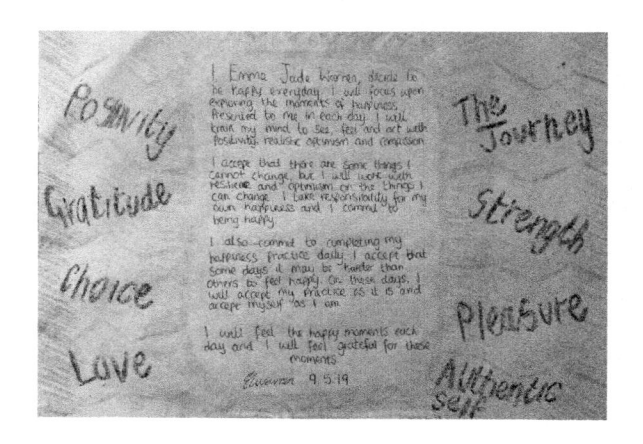

Taking Back Control- BPD

Build a support network

Having a written down support network can help you have a go-to support system in place.

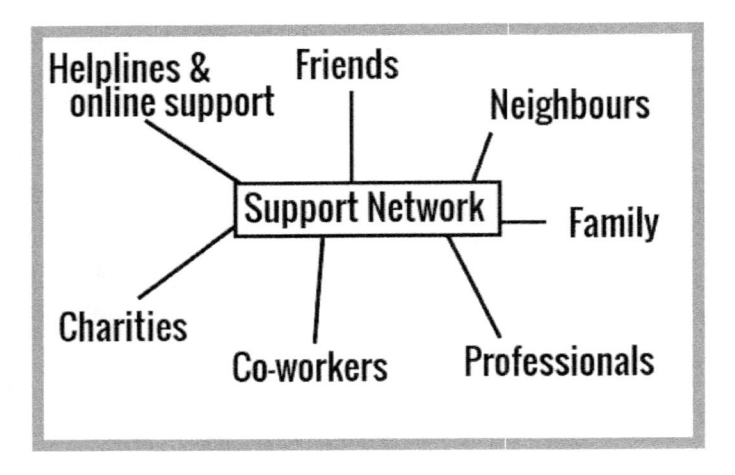

```
Helplines &      Friends
online support              Neighbours
         \      |      /
          Support Network —— Family
         /      |      \
   Charities    |        Professionals
           Co-workers
```

You may also find it useful to attach a list of helplines and online support resources, so they are on hand if you need to use them.

Here is a list of potentially useful helplines and online support websites.

Useful Helplines:

NHS Choices- 111
Samaritans- 116 123
Youth Access- 020 8772 9900
Clam- 0800 58 58 58
Mood Swings- 0161 832 3736
No Panic- 0300 7729 844
Rethink- 0300 5000 927
Lifecentre- 0808 802 0808
Refuge Domestic Abuse- 0808 2000 247
Drinkline- 0300 123 1110
FRANK- 0300 1236600

Taking Back Control- BPD

Useful online support:

www.borderlinearts.org
www.nhs.uk/using-the-nhs/nhs-services/mental-health-services
www.nhs.uk/oneyou/every-mind-matters
www. camhs.elft.nhs.uk
www.mind.org.uk
www.bpdworld.org
www.sane.org.uk
www.samaritans.org
www.lifesigns.org.uk
www.anxietyalliance.org
www.anxiety.org.uk
www.thecalmzone.net
www.moodswings.org.uk
www.nopanic.org.uk
www.mentalhealthmatters.com
www.rethink.org
www.lifecentre.uk.com
www.rapecrisis.org.uk
www.refuge.org.uk
www.survivorsuk.org
www.napac.org.uk
www.alcholics-anonymous.com
www.talktofrank.com
www.relate.org.uk

The Polar Bear Effect

The researcher, Wagner, conducted an experiment where he told people NOT to think of a white polar bear. If I said to you, do not think of a white polar bear... what are thinking about? A white polar bear!

In fact, Wagner's study confirmed that when we try not to think about something, ultimately, the more we think about it! So, what's the solution to this? If you don't want to think about something, how can you suppress these thoughts? Because of the attempt to suppress these thoughts, you are actually giving more power to them. You find yourself trying to force them away and then worsening your mental state when you come to realise they are still coming back in full force.

The solution is not to suppress these thoughts away, which is frustrating if you don't want them, but riding them out can make them feel less intensified. For example, if you're worried about an upcoming exam, the more you try and force yourself not to worry, the more you will worry and push yourself into an absolute frenzy about it. By simply accepting that you are feeling worried you give yourself more willpower to get through it. You stop trying to force the matter out of your head and in turn the matter stops pushing itself back into your head.

If you find that breaking the fight against your unwanted thoughts still isn't helping, there is also some other things you could try. Meditation is one, meditation has been proven to help people gain more control over their thoughts. You could also try distraction. The most crucial method is allocating worry time. By this you can free up your mind by promising to only worry about it at an allocated time.

Healing crystals

Jon is a buyer and seller of Quality Crystals. As a crystal healer he likes to do all he can to make sure he lays his hands on the best quality crystals he possibly can at competitive prices. All of his crystals are carefully chosen and purchased individually.

www.facebook.com/JonsCrystalHealing

The Benefits of Healing Crystals.
Written by Jon Martin

Crystals have been used for healing purposes for thousands of years, with historical references dating back as far as the Ancient Sumerians, the Ancient Egyptians, Incans, Mayans, Chinese... the list goes on. In fact, I challenge you to find any great historical civilisation that hasn't referenced the use of crystals for healing purposes of some sort. Can they all possibly be wrong?

I often get asked do crystals really work? Do they have real healing properties?

I have always been drawn to crystals and have drifted towards and away from them at different points in my life. Before I even had any real understanding of them, I often remember feeling more at ease by having simply carrying one on me. Did it make any logical sense? Probably not but I felt better having one on me.

So, what is the truth? My belief is that the power to overcome anything in your life is always held within you. Crystals are simply a tool that can help you tune in to the energies that can bring your own well-being back in to balance.

So how? Well simply put every crystal vibrates with its own unique energy frequency. The belief is that by being in their energy field we can be positively influenced by these energies and vibrations. These energies in turn interact with our own to help to rebalance our own aura, clearing any blockages from our Chakra's and helping to bring us back to a point of harmony. They can help us to heal physical, emotional, and psychological ailments, allow us to find our inner confidence, alleviate stress, fight fears, combat our addictions and help stabilise our insecurities.

As a crystal healer I have no doubt that crystals can be a beneficial health tool for anyone and everyone. I've seen the positive and sometimes life changing impacts in far too many people to have any doubt that they do indeed work.

Taking Back Control- BPD

Direct emotions outwardly not inwardly
If you're able to do so safely, directing your emotions outwardly instead of inwardly will help relieve emotion build-up.

- Express your anger physically and safely

- Cry out your pain in a safe space

- Comfort your inner child (cocoon yourself blanket, manage eating & sleeping, soothing music, self-compassion)

- Laugh freely

- Pour out heaps of love (For self & others)

- Free yourself (Forgive & let go, allow authentic self)

- Acceptance (Accept things you cannot change, allowance of feelings- it's ok not to be ok!)

- Express freely (sing/shout at the top of your lungs, dance like no-one is watching, creative expressive arts)

- Imagine (Imagine the person you feel the emotion for is in front of you and say what you would say as if they were there)

> *To live is to express oneself freely.*
> *Bruce Lee*

Dream journals & Lucid dreaming

Our opinions on dream interpretation vary. Some people believe that dreaming is your brains way of processing the days events, others believe that dreams reflect the way we are subconsciously feeling. Some researchers say that our dreams have no meaning or purpose. There is no research indicating the exact reason why we dream, although many theories have been suggested.

Dreaming, in my opinion, is curiously fascinating and I believe there is a lot we can learn about ourselves from our dreams. However, confusing, bizarre, happy, sad, scary or ridiculous dreams may be, maybe they hold the key to our subconscious. Theoretically, of course, dreams may hold answers that we are unable to access in our conscious state.

Keeping a dream journal next to your bed is a good idea if your want to start recoding and interpreting your dreams. We can very quickly forget our dreams when we wake, so keeping a pen and an open blank page at the ready might be an idea. Use your dream journal to write down anything you can remember; you may remember the full dream, or you may only remember snippets. Even if you don't remember much, it can still be helpful to write something down because you can use it to track how, when and what you dream on a regular basis and check for connections or similarities.

You may look at your dream journal and think, "that makes no sense to me". Learning how to interpret dreams requires you to think outside the box and find connections between the dream and your waking life.

Here is an example of a very strange dream I recently interpreted:

I'm in a living room environment, but I don't recognise the living room. There are two black two-seater leather sofas in the room, but I don't recall much else other than the blank white walls. I remember Finley's new schoolteacher there, although I don't recall how she got there. I'm trying to sit down on one of the sofas, but I keep sliding down and off it because they are leather. Then the schoolteacher bluntly says, "sit properly and sit still". I wanted to tell her that I couldn't and why, but for some reason I wasn't able to, which made me feel awful.

At first, it was a strange and bizarre dream, and I didn't understand what it was all about. On refection and a little thought, I was able to interpret why I dreamt it. My son, Finley, had just started school. Finley is Autistic and non-verbal. Although I was myself in the dream, on some level I wasn't, I was Finley. I was projecting my anxieties of him starting school and not being able to communicate with his new teacher. I'm unsure of what the white blank walls and black sofas were about. Maybe the white blank walls represented the new beginning, a clean slate, a space that had yet to be filled, maybe the black sofas represented the anxious feelings I had about it all.

What is lucid dreaming?

Lucid dreaming is when you are aware of what your dreaming and you recognise your thoughts and emotions. Whilst lucid dreaming you maybe able to intentionally change or take control of your dream. Having the abilities give you the option to alter bad dreams such as nightmares or reduce associated bad feelings about a situation. Lucid dreaming gives you the option to explore your own mind if done correctly.

How will I know that I am lucid dreaming?

You will be on some level consciously aware that you are in a dream. If you touch your own hand in a dream, it's likely that you won't feel the physical properties of it. Somewhat like, in films when a person tries to touch a ghost and their hand goes straight through them. You may also be able to tell because you are able to do things in a dream that you wouldn't be able to do in real-life, such as changing the environment, items or people. One interesting example I can give you, is when I dreamt, I was underwater and couldn't let myself breath for obvious reasons. However, just as in real-life, I eventually had to take a breath. I wasn't drowning, I was actually breathing underwater, at this point, even still in my dream state, I knew I was lucid dreaming because I was consciously controlling my thoughts and was aware of the fact that I was knew it was impossible to breath under water.

How can I experience lucid dreaming?

There isn't really any way of knowing how and if you will experience lucid dreaming. If were going to get a bit more technical about things, there are actually two types of sleep. NREM sleep (non-rapid eye movement) and REM sleep (Rapid eye movement). When we enter sleep, we enter into gradual NREM sleep where both our brains and bodies are in 'shutdown mode' and things like wound healing and new white blood cells are formed. After a period of NREM sleep only then do we enter into REM sleep where our brains become active and we experience dreams. NREM sleep is essential for bodies where-as REM sleep is classed as non-essential, however many would argue that we need REM sleep for our mental wellbeing.

Taking Back Control- BPD

There are no guarantees, but researchers have suggested, reducing caffeine intake, avoiding of electronics before bed, daily exercise and a relaxed sleep schedule will improve chances of lucid dreaming. If you're serious about improving your abilities to lucid dream you could also look at beginners' techniques in WBTB (Wake back to bed), MILD (Mnemonic induction of lucid dreams) and WILD (Wake-initiated lucid dream). (Source: https://www.healthline.com/health/what-is-lucid-dreaming#how-to-experience)

How is lucid dreaming relevant to helping my BPD?

Lucid dreaming gives us the opportunity to effectivity and safely explore our emotions. If we want to full on ugly cry whilst lucid dreaming, we can. If we want to go wild and trash something, we can. If we want to escape reality and go someplace else, we can. If we don't want to think, feel or be where we are whilst lucid dreaming, we can change it. In all, it can help us relieve some emotional tension or avoid it altogether if we want a break from it all.

Warning: While lucid dreaming is generally seen as safe, I would not advise purposely practicing lucid dreaming if you often experience depersonalisation, derealisation or dissociation due to the risk of increased confusion over reality and non-reality. In addition, if you experience any of the symptoms mentioned above at any time whilst purposely practicing, please discontinue the purposely practice of lucid dreaming.

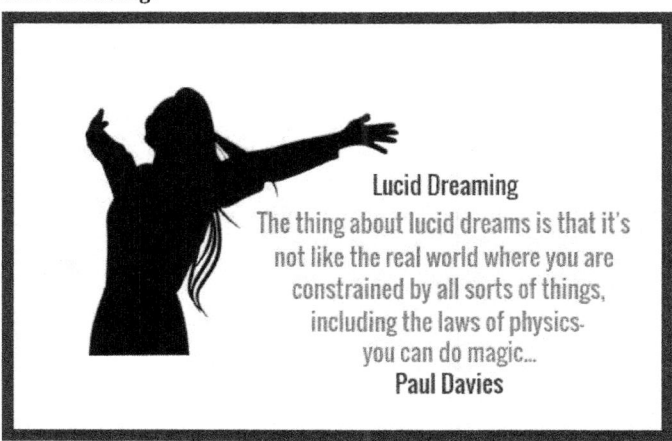

Lucid Dreaming
The thing about lucid dreams is that it's not like the real world where you are constrained by all sorts of things, including the laws of physics- you can do magic...
Paul Davies

Tidy house... Tidy mind

Tidy house, tidy mind is a well-known phase that does ring true for many with BPD. I am generally a well-organised, clean and tidy person. There's something about controlling the environment around me that enables me to feel more mentally in control too.

Having said this, I wanted to make an addition to the 'tidy house, tidy mind' theory. It isn't always easy to keep on top of everything going on in your daily life as well as keep a tidy house at the same time. I want to make the point that it's ok to let things go if you need to and to feel no guilt in doing this. Sometimes having the extra pressures of this will make us feel worse.

I guess it comes down to prioritising when needed. If you don't feel great today, maybe instead of washing the pots you can use the time effectivity to indulge in some self-care. Of course, the pots will still be there, waiting to be washed, but the dirty pots aren't hurting. Put yourself first and then fall back on the rule of tidy house... tidy mind.

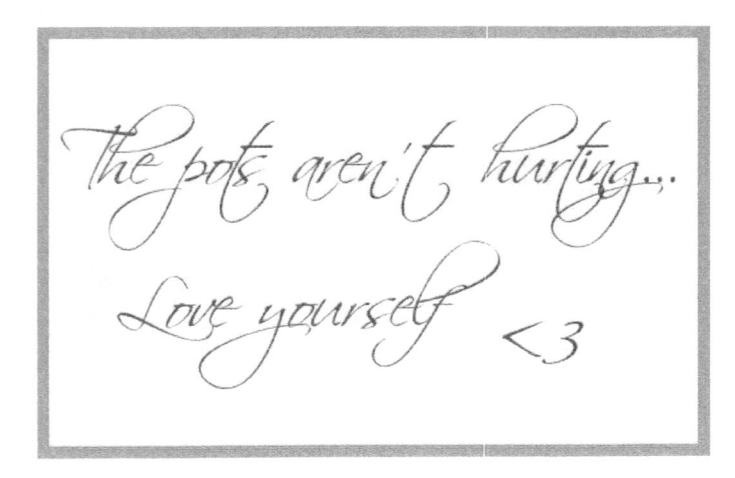

The pots aren't hurting...
Love yourself <3

Taking Back Control- BPD

A Positive reminder

Written By Emma Warren
(Pre-diagnosis, aged 25, 2017)

Keep positive, don't expect the worse.
Find courage, seek comfort, instead of the curse.
When things build up and you get stressed,
Remember you can't do it all but you can do your best.
See it as strength for it is not weakness,
Don't suppress just feel and process.
You are doing enough, you are enough,
Just take a moment to breathe when things get tough.

Acceptance/Riding it Out

I can find emotions very scary – and at times I feel like they will physically harm me, however this isn't true!

I am learning how important it is to let myself feel feelings (where appropriate), because other wise they build up, and I do sort of explode later on!

Ways which help me do this include:

* Acknowledging my emotions
* Riding out the emotion
* Breathing Deeply

Image curtesy of Sarah Eley

Harmful behaviours & Feeling Suicidal

Warning: this section may be upsetting; I have tried to keep it as informal and not triggering as is possible. It will mainly focus on coping techniques and useful information.

Self-harm can mean several things. There are many different ways this can be played out - essentially self-harm is any form of causing physical harm to yourself on purpose, however I don't want to go into too many details about different types of self-harm because it's an upsetting subject that maybe triggering for some readers.

I'm also aware that people self-harm for different reasons, some including, because they need to feel something or because of emotional overload. I don't claim to know the ins and outs of self-harm as I am not a psychologist. So please take my approaches to self-harm as something that might help you but also be aware that they might not. I'm going to share my experiences of steering myself away from self-harm and hopefully you can take something useful away from it.

At the time of my life when I was starting to become more self-aware, I wrote down this cycle in a little notebook. I had come to the realisation that my patterns of behaviour were going round in an endless cycle. I sat down and really thought about what happens to me and I how react as a result leading me to self-harm.

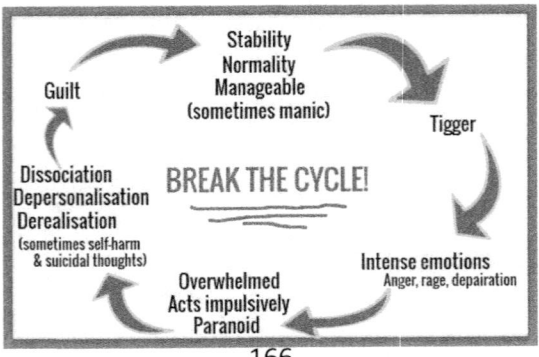

Cycle diagram:
- Stability / Normality / Manageable (sometimes manic)
- Tigger
- Intense emotions — Anger, rage, depairation
- Overwhelmed / Acts impulsively / Paranoid
- Dissociation / Depersonalisation / Derealisation (sometimes self-harm & suicidal thoughts)
- Guilt
- **BREAK THE CYCLE!**

I knew I needed to break the cycle if I could, but the question was how? The more I thought about it, the more I realised that I already knew how, and it wasn't a question of how. It came down to actually remembering to put into place the things I knew whilst I was in that state of mind, which was really the hard part!

First, learn to recognise your emotions, then STOP! Breath through it, give yourself time to think, move to a safe place if necessary. Second, manage your emotions, you are allowed to feel the emotions, however, learning to express the emotions safely is important. Thirdly, focus on trying to distract yourself by giving yourself an expressional outlet.

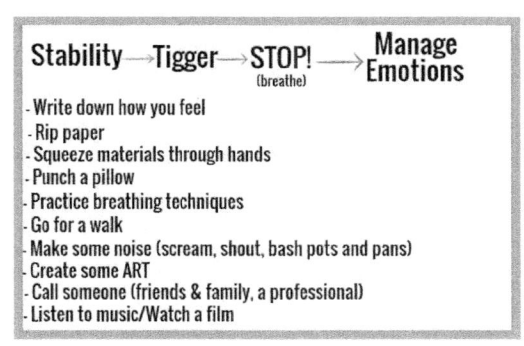

Stability → Tigger → STOP! (breathe) → Manage Emotions

- Write down how you feel
- Rip paper
- Squeeze materials through hands
- Punch a pillow
- Practice breathing techniques
- Go for a walk
- Make some noise (scream, shout, bash pots and pans)
- Create some ART
- Call someone (friends & family, a professional)
- Listen to music/Watch a film

I'm not saying that this is some sort of miraculous cure when it comes to self-harm, but it is something that has helped me. It gets easier with understanding and practice. It may not be what works for you, try it and see what you think. I am able to prevent my emotions spiralling out of control and escalating to self-harm. I remember to STOP! Breath... and manage.

* Ride it out.
Strong emotional reactions (and the urges to self harm, binge or drink) usually last for a few minutes and then begin to subside. Set a timer for 10 minutes and practice riding out the emotion.

Image curtesy of Sarah Eley

Suicidal thoughts

No one likes to talk about suicide, but in the not talking it's becoming a controversial topic and creating challenging barriers for people to reach out and ask for help.

I have experienced suicidal thoughts and I know what it's like to feel like no-one around you understands. It's like being stuck in a big black void of space alone and you don't not how to get out or if you even have the energy to get out.

I urge anyone with signs of suicidal thoughts to be brave, reach out and ask for help. It isn't an easy thing to do, granted, but having support in place is halfway to recovery. If you think someone you know is feeling suicidal, please reach out to them in a non-judgmental and unpressured way. Give them permission to openly express how they are feeling with you. Provide empathy and avoid telling them why they shouldn't be feeling like this.

In my personal experience of feeling suicidal, I was in an open discussion about how I was feeling with a family member. The family member mentioned that my twenty-first birthday was coming up in a few days, so I had that to look forward to. I instantly felt worse! It was my twenty-first birthday but the last thing on my mind was celebrating this. It reinforced the feelings having nothing to live for and I found myself comparing my life to others of the same age. 'Others' would see their twenty-first birthday as a major milestone in their lives and celebrate this with friends as transition from adolescence to adulthood.

1) I didn't have any friends to celebrate with.

2) I wasn't ready for the transitional period to take effect.

3) I thought it was pointless given that fact that I didn't want to live my life anymore anyway.

I am not in any way trying to shame or blame my family member for unintentionally making me feel worse. It was said out of love and concern. I just wanted to really demonstrate how choice of words must be thought about when you are trying to say something.

Non triggering suggestions:

Invite them to talk.

I noticed you are feeling a bit down lately, I'm here to listen if you want to talk about anything.

Ask them to elaborate.

What has happened to make you feel this way?

Do you know why this has happened?

Empathise

I'm so sorry that this is happened to you.

I'm sorry you are feeling this way, it must be awful.

Shift their attention to support. (avoid asking them directly to get support as this can make them feel pressured)

If there's anything I can do to help, I'm always here.

Is there anything you can think of that we can do together to help alleviate some of your emotional pain?

Would you like me to help you look into support or things that may help?

What can we do right now so that you are safe?

Taking Back Control- BPD

Some warning signs of suicide include:

- feelings of despair, pessimism, hopelessness, desperation.
- recent self-injury behaviours.
- withdrawal from social circles.
- sleep problems.
- increased use of alcohol or other drugs or overeating.
- winding up affairs or giving away prized possessions.
- threatening suicide or expressing a desire to die.
- talking about "when I am gone".
- talking about voices that tell him or her to do something dangerous.
- having a plan and the means to carry it out.

Reference: CAMH

If you or someone you know is in crisis or emergency, dial 999. 999 calls are not just for physical emergencies!

Support

If you or someone you know is struggling with self-harm or suicidal thoughts, here is a list of places where you can find support.

SelfHarmUK

SelfHarmUK is a project supporting young people who are affected by self-harm. They offer a safe space providing support, answering questions and pointing you in the right direction.

www.selfharm.co.uk

Young Minds

Young Minds is the UK's leading charity providing emotional and wellbeing support for children and young people. They also have an array of support information for parents.

www.youngminds.org.uk
0808 802 5544

Life Signs

Life signs is on online support platform for self-injury guidance and network support. Their website has many helpful suggestions and coping techniques to anyone who needs it.

www.lifesigns.org.uk

Beating Eating Disorders

Beating Eating Disorders has been a UK charity since 1989. Committed to end the pain and suffering caused by eating disorders. Their website had a very detailed wealth of support information.

www.beateatingdisorders.org.uk

Samaritans

The Samaritans respond to calls for help every 7 seconds! They offer a non-judgmental, no pressure way to get in contact and talk. You can contact Samaritans to talk about anything that might be troubling you. Here's how to connect with Samaritans:

Free phone: 116 123
Email: jo@samaritans.org
Write a letter:
Chris
Freepost RSRB-KKBY-CYJK
PO Box 9090
STIRLING FK8

Alternatively, you can download the app which is full of self-help suggestions, coping strategies and how to stay safe in a crisis. You can also, track your mood, create a safety plan and keep track of helpful activities.

Taking Back Control- BPD

Taking Back Control- BPD

Chapter 6- Taking back control and making something beautiful with BPD

"It is our choices, Harry, that show what we truly are, far more than our abilities,"- J.K. Rowling- Harry Potter and the chamber of secrets.

Taking Back Control- BPD

Intro...

Welcome to the final chapter of this book, so far, we've looked at the following:

- Self-care
- Self-talk
- Coping techniques for generalised mental health
- Creative Expressive Arts
- Self-doubt vs self-belief
- Recognising and managing BPD emotions

This chapter focuses on bringing all these together in support of your journey to be the best you that you can be. At the very start of the book it was said that I believe that BPD is nothing to fear, instead embraced! We will now look at this in more detail, firstly by introducing you to the 1-2-3 technique, secondly by looking at the benefit of daily practices and finally by looking ahead to your future goals.

The 1-2-3 Technique

The 1-2-3 technique is something I put together for myself, although this may be similar to other strategies, I feel that the format I've has drawn up for this technique offers a simple and effective method that I found worked for me. When I first realised I had the tools I needed to help improve my own life I also found that they were a scramble in my head and there was no real instruction, from what I could find, that simply put these tools into a method that was easy to remember and practice. I struggled immensely with my anxiety and avoided most social situations. Once I formulated the technique, I started to see results over time and it changed my life!

Like any set of practices, this too requires practice and it's important to remember that every small step is a step forward. It can take time but what you put into it is what you will get out of it. Its time frame is not a priority, using it at a pace that you feel comfortable with is.

Important: Please note that this method is used as a sort of problem-solving tool when it comes to your behaviour, thoughts and feelings surrounding a situation. It is not a meant as means to cure mental illness or to control extreme emotional and/or deep-rooted traumas. If this is your case, then please consult your doctor or seek professional help. It is also not a one size fits all solution, although helpful in many situations, it is not advised to be used in potentially harmful or unsafe circumstances.

Taking Back Control- BPD

The technique is simply the act of initiating change into your everyday situations. It's about taking back control and learning from these new experiences you can create. Over time it gets easier and your personal growth improves. You will also learn more about yourself as you focus on changing and embracing experiences. You can do this and you have the potential for change, dedicate yourself to the learning process you will see more and more improvement which will in turn will give you more confidence and motivation to continue. Once you see it as a learning process you can tackle any situation head on.

Applying the technique to your situations...

1. Assessment

Assessing the situation is the first stage and it's about becoming aware of your emotional state and physical behaviours. Notice how you are feeling and why it is you might be feeling this way. If there are others in the situation, notice their behaviour and consider why they might be behaving how they are. This stage is all about observation so you can recognise how the situation makes you feel. Learning about how you react to situations can help you change these reactions as you move forward. It will also teach you to become aware of your thought processes and how you can vanish negative thoughts from the offset to maintain positivity whilst finding resolution. Believe us that this does become easier over time.

Always remember to be mindful of your self-talk during the assessment and be kind to yourself. This is a new experience, and it can be quite challenging the first couple of times. If you find your thoughts are negative at this time, try not to criticise yourself for this but try and replace some of these thoughts with things like:

It's understandable that I feel this way.
These thoughts about myself are reflective of my past but do not define who I am today.
I am safe.
I recognise that I feel negativity at this time, but I choose not to give power to unhelpful thoughts.
I allow myself the opportunity to leave these thoughts in the past and concentrate on the present moment.
I accept that I'm experiencing difficulties with my situation, but I understand that I need to recognise that there is a need for change.
I know that I need to become aware that my thoughts and feelings are causing me distress so I can use these to change direction and move on.
I will remember that this is a new experience to which I must allow myself time to learn how to use the technique effectivity.

It's important to also be aware of any physical symptoms so you can take control over these and avoid things such as becoming disorientated or finding yourself in a state of panic. You may find recapping over the coping techniques and managing emotions useful. If you start to become aware that your negative responses are triggered by either past trauma's, your insecurities or fear of judgment, that's okay, just accept that is why you are feeling this way and be kind to yourself. Yes, these things have been a problem in the past, but that is where they are... in the past. Keep your mind focused on the present, the present situation, your present observation in your assessment. The point of observation is not to make judgement on yourself or others. Think of it as if you're looking down on the situation from above, viewing it from a different vantage point. This can help give you perspective of the situation. Decide whether you are looking it from all angles or if you are stuck in one viewpoint. If you can't see another angle, don't be too hard on yourself, after all this is your only known view to date. Your mind is used to the same pattern of thinking but if you really open yourself up to observation and look for perspective you can change these thinking patterns.

2. Accept or Change *(Two options.)*

Option 1- Accept: Certain situations cannot be changed because they are out of your control. Acceptance is key here even though it is not always easy. Again, here you should be mindful of your self-talk and be careful not blame yourself. It's situation dependent on how you should use your self-talk but try comforting things like:

It's okay, I'm okay and I accept that I cannot change this situation.
There was nothing more I could have done, I accept this, and I can try again next time.
I am a strong and resilient person. I have the courage to accept things I cannot change and the capability to move forward.
I accept that my current emotional state is not good right now, but I am okay in this moment and this is good enough. I accept that I cannot change this right now, but I know my emotional state will improve again.
I accept that I do not have control over this situation and some things are just out of my hands, but I choose to feel okay about it.
It isn't my fault; it isn't anyone's fault, but I accept that this is what has happened.
It's okay that I couldn't change the situation this time but I recognise what could have been done differently and I can change the next similar situation.

For me, I find there is something quite freeing in the words "I accept", it's like you've allowed yourself to let go and feel okay about the situation. Remember to do just this, let the situation go, just let it go. It is unchangeable so you shouldn't linger over the what if's, these thoughts do not serve you.

Option 2- Change: This the more creative option of the two, this is the one that gives you the power. Yes, that's right, the power! Try saying to yourself a few times, "I have the power!" Do try to take yourself seriously and not believe you are doing an impersonation of Bruce almighty! Did you find it empowering? Or did you find yourself saying it but not really believing it? You have all the power and you're in total control here. By completing your assessment, you will have now become more self-aware of your feelings regarding your situation. From this you can now decide how you choose to feel instead. I realise that it may sound too simple or unbelievable at this point. By saying I choose to feel

Taking Back Control- BPD

calm about the situation gives that thought power even if you usually you would be quick to anger. You bypass becoming angry because you have done your assessment and decided that this time you are going to change that. Choose how to feel, you choose and then say this repeatedly a couple of times in your head. Still not convinced? To back up your choice of feeling you need to choose a behaviour, or reaction or resolution that matches your feeling. It isn't just in the thinking; it's also in the doing. I understand that the doing is the hard part. It can be scary but remind yourself that you need to be the change you wish to see even if this means breaking out of your comfort zone once in a while. Also remember that this does not have to be everything at once, choose one thing to change and you have laid a foundation to build on next time. Rome wasn't built in a day! Here are some phases of encouragement you may wish to say to yourself:

I am an assertive person and I choose to change my situation.
I believe I can change this situation because I am in control.
I have the courage to be brave and venture out of my comfort zone every now and again.
By changing my situation, I am taking control and learning I can do this.
I'm creating new experiences and, in the process, removing bad associations I previously felt surrounding the situation.... Or... I'm replacing any bad expectations of the situation with good expectations.
I trust myself and my choices.
I recognise the power within me to change this.
I'm determined I can accomplish this.
I let go of negative thoughts and I choose only positive thoughts to hold on to.
I know that in order to achieve the change I wish to see I need to complete my chosen behaviour, reaction or resolution.
I remember that even little changes provide a foundation to build on when moving forward.
I remain motivated and confident in my abilities.

You need to be patient with yourself in this process as it is a really challenging thing to go against your usual thought and behavioural patterns. It can take time to get used to it all, you are trying to retrain how your mind has been working for many years. This takes daily practice, but it is possible to make these changes.

3. Evaluation

The evaluation is an important stage. The more you do the technique, the more you learn. Always start by praising yourself, be proud of yourself and find the rewards. It is not an easy thing to do so you really must take the time to appreciate your efforts. When evaluating your situation ask yourself questions and really consider your answers.

- How did it make you feel at the time?
- Did your physical symptoms go away, increase or stay the same?
- How are feeling now?
- Do you feel accomplished?
- Do you feel like you've resolved the situation, or will it require more attention?
- Will you need to apply the action again? Is it a reoccurring situation?
- When do you think you will use it again? And will you need to do anything in addition?
- How do you think it went in general?
- Is there anything you could have done differently?
- Do you feel like something worked well?
- Do you feel like anything didn't work?
- Do you feel more confident to try the 1-2-3 Technique again?

Evaluating is about learning from your experience. What can you take from it and what do you want to leave behind? These answers will help you when you want to try the 1-2-3 Technique again. Every time you go to use the technique you will use it more effectively and it will eventually require little to no assessment as you will perform your change instinctively.

The "clause" part

Knowing when to walk away...

It is from my experiences of using the technique that I has come to realise that some situations can't be resolved, particularly the ones involving others. Walking away does not mean that you have failed, and it does not give you permission to be hard on yourself. You have to re-track back a little and use the acceptance part of the technique for cases like these. You can however still take something from this. Sometimes it is okay to walk away and, in these cases, it is often the right thing to do. It is your judgement to make, trust your judgment because you know what's best for you. Take what you can from it and move on. I understand this is quite a confusing addition to the technique to make sense of, but it really **refers to anything that compromises your safety or wellbeing in any way.**

The 1-2-3 Technique

1- Assessment
2- Accept or change
3- Evaluation

This technique ties everything together from the book. So, there is a lot of factors to consider.

It all just takes PRACTICE and the LOVE to do it for yourself.

I PROMISE it does get easier.

Everything becomes a way of life, a lifestyle change.

It isn't always going to be referring back to things to know what to do next.

You learn it, you keep it, you live it.

You TAKE BACK CONTROL...
You make your life beautiful...

Gratitude's

Gratitude's are great way to bring positivity into your life. It's so easy to focus on the things you haven't got rather than the things that you have got. Practicing gratitude's allows a person to focus solely on the positives within their life.

My experience of gratitude's allows the practice of focusing on the positives within my life. I first started practicing gratitude's after I stumbled upon a guided gratitude meditation audio online. Since hearing the audio I have practiced my own gratitude meditations. These involve speaking out loud the things in which I am grateful for. As I mentioned in chapter 2, 'bedtime sensory', bedtime is great time practice gratitude's because you can include your daily positives.

Being grateful is really down your matter of perspective, a small thing for someone else may be a big thing you. Big or small, or however insignificant you might feel about something, if it brings a little positivity your way there really is no wrong ideas, positives don't have to be big. You can practice gratitude's wherever and whenever you like. You may wish to write them down, or you may wish to say them out loud like I do. You do what you prefer and whatever feels comfortable.

In conclusion, gratitude's are great and bring your attention to shifting away from focusing on the negatives by focusing on the positives instead.

What are you grateful for?

Rituals

When I say rituals, I don't mean in the religious or traditional sense. 'My rituals', if you like, are little instances we create and repeat within our lives. I suppose you could almost say it's a little like a routine, however, it isn't structured and resisted in the same way. For example, it isn't like the routine of setting an alarm to get out of bed in the morning. Think of them more like nuggets of happiness, think about things that you enjoy and do on a regular basis. Chances are you may have your own little rituals going already, or maybe you don't and that is fine. Rituals are similarly relatable to examples in the self-care chapter, however, the difference is that rituals become more incorporated into our regular daily lifestyles, where-as, self-care is something we must make or set aside the time for.

The benefits of rituals maximise our mental wellbeing. As well as keeping our minds relaxed and stress-free, rituals also help us to connect on a deeper level to ourselves and the universe. Drawing in positive energy and releasing positive energy back out into the universe. Thus, creating a tranquil and safe warmth of energy to go about your day.

I will tell you a little about my daily rituals to demonstrate what exactly I mean when I say 'My rituals'. I want to emphasise that rituals should not be over complicated and should come naturally. Most importantly, they should be enjoyed and spark a burst of positive energy into your day.

Taking Back Control- BPD

Emma's rituals include:

- Taking my dog a walk each morning after I have dropped my son off at school. After the busy rush of the morning, I find it helps to slow the mind and body back down before returning home and continuing my day with a refreshed mindset to focus on my university studies. Additionally, I enjoy the quiet and visual niceties of the woodland walks surrounding my house.

- Singing whilst driving! I love my music (and singing of course), I often listen to positive music whilst driving to my destination because it's a chunk of time that can be used effectively to express my love for music and in the process channel all that positive energy. Tip: Proud by Heather Small is great for this!

- I use affirmation cards daily by turning over a card which contains a thought to meditate and focus on throughout the day. Using the cards help me to pause and reflect on the here and now. Affirmations set intentions for the day and remind me of the positives that I already know, but sometimes forget.

- Weekend food is always a well-loved ritual for me. I have my son throughout the week and at the weekend, he goes to his other parents' house. With my son having ASD, he is a very fussy eater and I find myself cooking the same food week in, week out. It's a very bland diet which mostly consists of pasta and bread! At the weekend, I make it a ritual to not only cook and eat my food but to thoroughly enjoy a meal with flavor and spice.

Long-term Goals

Having long-term goals are something we aspire to throughout our lives. It is our 'pursuit to happiness' that drives us to do and become the person we wish to be. Long-term goals can bring feelings of purpose, meaning and validation for us.

Long-term goals can fill us with many expectations of ourselves which can be hard to meet. Placing them out of reach making us doubt our abilities to achieve success.

YOU ─────────────────────────── GOAL

Setting small and realistic achievable goals is the way forward. By setting smaller goals we are more able to continue on-track to reach the end goal. Breaking it down and having it in small chunks makes life more manageable. Try to avoid where possible setting time limits if you're able to because if we aren't able to meet the deadline it forces extra pressure onto us and affects our mental wellbeing. Remember to acknowledge your small achievements as well as the big ones.

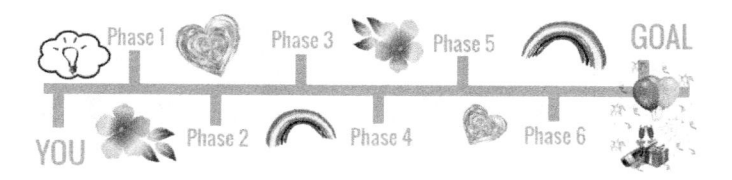

YOU — Phase 1 — Phase 2 — Phase 3 — Phase 4 — Phase 5 — Phase 6 — GOAL

-What's the most important thing for me in this moment?

Achieving long-term goals is about natural progression.

We can't complete phase 2 before we've completed phase 1.

And...

We can't give something we haven't got...

This means, that we must take the time to evaluate our core needs before we add any external pressures. Think about what the most important thing for you in this moment is, if this means waiting to complete your next phase then give yourself the time to regenerate first.

Reflection is a valuable tool to help us make the most of our time. Either reflecting on what you might do differently next time or by reflecting on how your feel, just like in the 1-2-3 technique. Keeping feelings in check can help us establish a pattern that works. So, for instance, if you're starting to feel run down, maybe pause or reduce your workload.

YOU CANT POUR FROM AN EMPTY CUP

ELEANOR BROWNN

-Qualities and strengths

Recognising your qualities and strengths can play a big part in your abilities to do something. We all have things we're good at, they may be different from what other people are good at but regardless we can work with what we have to be the best version of ourselves. It draws upon being self-aware and really harnessing what you have to offer. Celebrate your qualities and strengths because they make you who you are, and they are also unique to you.

It's important to allow yourself room to grow. This is not about pointing out weaknesses in yourself, it's about thinking what improvements you might want to make. Personal growth is important and never ending, this, is a good thing! We can grow throughout our lives, add to our qualities and strengths and progress to thrive.

-Without fear where would I be?

I'm going this leave this question here for you to ponder on. It's an interesting question, of course we'll never know when it comes to our past, but remember, we can be whoever we want to be today. Whatever you just envisioned, it's achievable, you got this!

One final note on long term goals!
Always remember to be SAFE!

- S- Small achievable goals
- A- Assess and reflect
- F- Find qualities and strengths
- E- Encouraging and reassuring self-talk is a must!

Taking back control and making something beautiful

Lets just take a moment here to just breathe and reflect. This book has been at times a lot to take in and somewhat intense....

Our mental and physical well-being present a complex range of factors that we are always trying to keep in check and balance. It can be mentally and physically exhausting and we often don't give ourselves enough credit for managing our everyday lives.

This final section of the book is about taking back control and making something beautiful. The beauty really lies in the simplicity of the calm, the sanctuary of security and the delight of love.

We are beautiful
Our lives are beautiful
Other people are beautiful
The world is beautiful

The beauty is there, we don't need to find it, we just need to see it, to feel it and as the title would suggest, to make it. Making beauty doesn't mean that beauty doesn't already exist, it means that we can create more, and who wouldn't want more? Right?

Taking Back Control- BPD

By choosing to take back control we invite more beauty into ourselves, into our lives and into our futures. As we learn, grow, overcome, achieve, feel more love, give more love, live the life we want to without compromise... and so on.

This book encompasses everything you need to start your journey into taking back control. This isn't to say that you will need it all though, if you can take at least one thing from this book that helps you then I'll have accomplished what I set out to do. My focal point of writing this book is to make support for mental health readily accessible, whether that be for BPD/EUPD, ASD, OCD anxiety, depression and just about anything you can think of that refers to mental health. The book is primarily aimed at BPD/EUPD because I, Emma, am aware of it's challenges and I have made changes to ensure that it lives with me and not I live with it.

Confused?

Taking Back Control- BPD

Let me explain...

BPD doesn't define me, label me or reduce the quality of my life. I don't put up with BPD, I don't live with BPD having control over my life. I invite/accept BPD into my life, I learn how to make BPD work for me.

I get emotional, that's a given, but I control my emotions, they do not control me.

I learn that I am more capable of feeling deeply, but I choose to give power to my positive feelings and drown out the negative ones. In doing so, putting positivity into the universe and drawing positivity back.

I see myself as sociable but also know when I need space, and I am happy to give myself this.

I know I'm different, but I see this a good thing, and I won't change for anyone or anything.

Just like everyone, I have my blips, but I rise to the challenges, they're really an opportunity to learn and grow.

I don't feel compromised in anyway because I know my deep-rooted emotions only enhance my motivation and drive in life. I know I am very strong, and I see my potential.

I channel my positivity which is only magnified when I use my tunnel vision or black and white splitting, all or nothing. It's *'all white'* in the case of these terminologies. I make my own terminology... *'all colour'*

We feel in colour!

Taking Back Control- BPD

I take my self-love and self-care very seriously and I experience these with pride and admiration for myself.

I believe in myself, even when I don't. I self-doubt but I take control and remind myself to believe. I do not give in.

I'm impulsive but not unhealthy or harmfully. I impulsively, or maybe a better word is spontaneously, do things to enhance my life experiences or add magic to my days.

I make my own identity, and I am happy with who I am. Even if this means switching between masculine and feminine appearances.

I use creative outlets for my emotions because sometimes I need to expel negativity and make room for more positivity. My 'safe' extreme emotional outlets mean that I'm a talented and creative person.

I am able to empathise more with others and see things from an entirely different stance. Which in turn makes me a non-judgment person and extremely understanding.

When I love, I so do whole-heartedly which means that my relationships are something truly unique and special.

I am an interesting person due to my more diverse and broad range of life experience.

I can connect on a higher level spiritually because I can feel emotion deeply and openly, especially during meditation.

I can be an energetic person, meaning that sometimes

Taking Back Control- BPD

I experience manic episodes, but I do so without the negative traits associated with it. I recognise my elevation in mood and use this to enhance my positive orientations or my involvement in pleasurable activities.

BPD is nothing to fear, instead embraced.

Invite/accept our BPD into your lives...

We don't live with BPD... BPD lives with us!

Taking Back Control- BPD

Taking Back Control- BPD

Love for
Autism Spectrum Disorder

Love for ASD

Autism Spectrum Disorder is becoming more recognised and more commonly diagnosed. ASD is massive part of my personal life. A friend of mine was originally diagnosed as Asperger's although in more recent years the separate autism diagnosis is no longer categorised in this way. You may have heard autism referred to in the following:

- Classic Autism
- Severe Autism
- Asperger's Syndrome
- Childhood Autism
- High functioning Autism

You also may have heard these sub-categories too:

- PDA- Pathological Demand Avoidance
- Pervasive Development Disorder
- Global Development Delay
- Speech and Language Delay
- Rett's Syndrome

There maybe more that you know that I have not listed, however, despite previous complex and confusing categories, all types of autism are now universally known as **Autism Spectrum Disorder.** This may be something which you already know but I just wanted to make clear that this section is aimed at anyone on the spectrum, diagnosed or undiagnosed and for anyone supporting someone with ASD, like myself.

I am not a qualified psychologist, pediatrician or Doctor. I am a mother who has a child with ASD and although I have an accredited certificate in Understanding Autism, my knowledge and experience is subject to my personal autism journey with my son.

This is my gorgeous four-year-old son, Finley and I. Finley was diagnosed ASD at two-years-old, he is (at the present moment) completely non-verbal. Communication as you can imagine has been a challenging aspect of our everyday lives. I've received very little support in terms of psychological, behavioural and speech and language therapies since his diagnosis two years ago. As a mother, I have stopped at nothing to make this world a place where my boy can feel welcomed and happy. My research has steered me into natural and holistic approaches as well as various forms of visual and communication aids. Slowly but surely, we are finding things that work for us.

Natural and Holistic approaches:

The Nemechek Protocol, by Dr. Nemechek

The Nemechek Protocol has four simple but effective steps, repair, reverse, restore and maintain which controls inflammation, and strengthens both neurological and immune systems. Its treatment consists of small daily dosages of fish oil, pure extra virgin olive oil and inulin.

The protocol has made such a difference to Finley, his focus increased, and his hyperactivity calmed. He is also attempting to say a couple of words! Please do **consult your Doctor or Pediatrician before administering the treatment.**

To find out more you can purchase Dr. Nemechek's book which will explain everything you need to know and where to go should you need further advice: *The Nemechek Protocol for autism and developmental disorders: A How-To Guide For Restoring Function.* (Dr. Patrick M. Nemechek D.O. and Jean R. Nemechek J.D.)

Earthing & Grounding

I purchased Finley a Earthing sleep mat from: www.groundology.co.uk
They do a range of grounding products, not just sleep mats. The products enhance our grounding input which improves sleep, reduces stress and increases feelings of calm. It's all about drawing natural energy from the earth. Connecting to the earth results in positive charges and brings inner balance. You can ground without purchasing products by connecting yourself to nature, walking barefoot outside and touching plants and trees. This is where the term tree hugging stems from and we do enjoy a spot tree hugging every now and again. Love the earth and it will love you back!

Creative Expressive Arts/ Messy Play

CEA can be great for anyone of any age. Finley loves messy play, so we incorporate the two and he gets his sensory input. He is a very sensory orientated child!

Pets

Pets can offer invaluable therapy and love. We have a dog named Bear. His name is actually one of the few words that Finley can physically say. Bear is always there for cuddles or play. I love to watch the bond between the pair grow and grow. Bear has really made a difference in Finley's life.

Visual and Communication Aids

Picture Exchange Communication System

PECS is visual aid where pictures are used to communicate the needs/wants and then exchanged for the needs/wants. So, Finley would bring a picture of, let's say for example, a banana. I would then exchange the picture (take the picture card) for a banana (give him a banana). Please note, that I do not use the official PECS cards, every visual communication aid has been replicated and homemade. Visit: www.mypecs.com where there is a library of free resources and ideas.

Timetables

I also use a timetable with Finley, I'm putting an image in to demonstrate this. The first example reads as- When we wake up, we will get dressed and eat breakfast which today is crumpets. Then it's time to play, mummy will play with you.

The second example reads as- When we get home, you can watch TV, then we will have something to eat. Then it's bath time, afterwards, we will put pajamas on and go to sleep.

Tip: It's great to use real photos of people and not just a standard a 'mummy picture card' so it can be easily recognised by the user.

First and second visual

Sometimes in order to explain the logical order of things to Finley, I use the first and second visual. As pictured here, Finley would ask for something to eat and I wouldn't be able to exchange the card for the desired item because at this moment, it's time to try and go toilet. So, to help Finley to understand, I use the visual. Saying no or trying to explain via talking isn't something that Finley can easily understand. With this, he can clearly see that he will get what he wants but first he must go toilet.

Taking Back Control- BPD

Visual communicate cards

Similar to the PECS cards but these don't require an exchange of an item. These cards can be used to show the user or used by the user to communicate. We don't use these often, they are not our preferred method of communication but that doesn't mean that they don't work for others. It's about finding what works for you.

Taking Back Control- BPD

Makaton signing

Makaton signing is our preferred method of communication. We use signing so much now that we hardly ever need to use the cards or visual systems anymore. My Makaton is self-taught through YouTube videos and I've just passed this on to Finley. Over time, we've learned enough to be able to use this as our main method of communication. Finley has even invented some of his own signs and mummy had to learn from him too!

Here is our activity blog if you would like to see it, there is a range of activities that are suitable for ASD children.

www.finleyjacob16.wixsite.com/childrensactivities

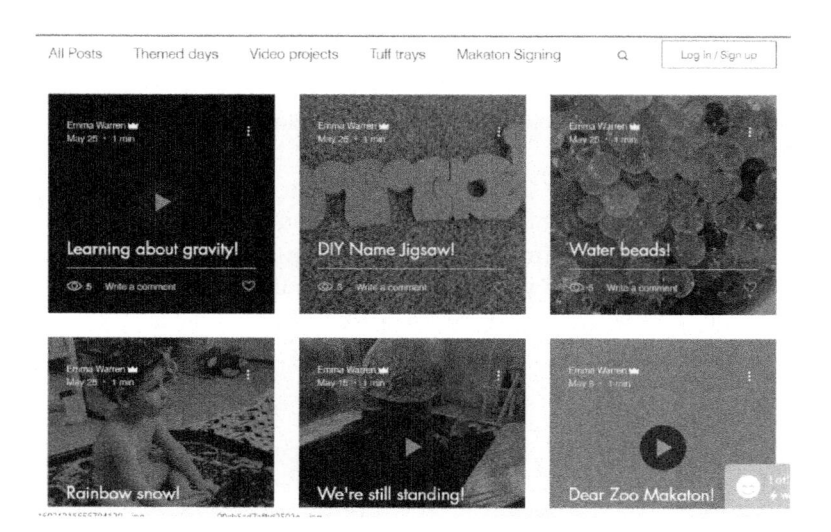

I don't pretend to have all the answers on ASD. Our ASD journey is only the tip of iceberg when it comes to the spectrum, but I wanted to share this incase it can be of help to anyone else. I believe, ASD just like BPD is not definitive of a person and it doesn't impact on quality of life. Having ASD means you see you world differently. I don't believe in bringing Finley into my world of seeing the world from a neurotypical point of view. Instead, I learn to see the world as he does, I'm not always able to do this, but I try, and I know Finley does too. We try together on our ASD journey!

I want to take this opportunity to reach out to anyone with ASD or has someone in their lives with ASD. It's a learning experience that can be very hard and challenging at times. The outside world isn't always accepting and doesn't at times understand...

but...

I do!

And so do many other people in the same boat.

Please reach out to support groups in person or online. They do help, ASD support groups provide and understanding and non-judgmental platform for you get things of your chest, ask for advice and so much more. The ASD community has your back!

Useful Autism Links

www.autism.org.uk

www.nhs.uk/conditions/autism/support

www.childautism.org.uk
Helpline: 01344 8822 48

www.youtube.com/TheNemechekProtocol/about

www.youtube.com/SingingHandsUK

www.signalongwithus.co.uk

www.britishsignlanguage.com

www.autismspeaks.org

www.exploreyoursenses.co.uk

www.specialneedstoys.com/uk

Talking of online ASD support groups...
I came across a poem that a member of an ASD group had posted. It was so relatable, real and inspiring. It touched me. I approached (through private message) the author and explained to her how I connected with her words and that I thought other people would too. The author, Adrienne Mason, has kindly given permission for me to share the poem with you and I hope you find it as heartwarmingly beautiful and relatably reassuring as I did.

Author Bio

Adrienne Mason is a community worker for a mental health charity in North East England. She lives with her husband and two sons aged 8 and 4.

Adrienne's youngest son Tommy has ASD, although it was oldest son Harley who was the inspiration behind the poem as he was asked to write a poem for his school homework about a family member and wanted to write about his brother.

Initially Adrienne intended only to write a few lines to start the poem but found the words and feelings just kept coming and she was unable to stop writing.

After showing the poem to a few people and receiving positive feedback, Adrienne felt that perhaps this poem could benefit others who may share the same feelings and emotions about their ASD children.

Tommy is...
By Adrienne Mason

Tommy is a ball of fire.
Tommy is full of desire.
Tommy is a little rock,
Tommy is an odd sock.
Tommy finds words hard to say,
Tommy tries hard every day.
Tommy loves to act things out,
Tommy gets upset you can hear him shout.
Tommy is mischievous with a grin on his face,
Tommy runs away like he's competing in a race.
Tommy hears rules but can't always follow,
Tommy finds repercussions cause stress & sorrow.
Tommy may ignore you as if he doesn't care,
Tommy's brain works differently but he knows that you are there.
Tommy isn't keen on sharing things with girls or boys,
Tommy would rather play alone independently with his toys.
Tommy can get violent and this makes me so sad,
Tommy doesn't know his strength we never would stay mad.
Tommy is very loving he will give & take affection,
Tommy's mood can change in a second & make you feel rejection.
Tommy is growing up & older he will get,
Tommy will face boundaries of which he hasn't yet.
Tommy loves his family & with their help will strive,
Tommy may be different but he is very much alive.
Tommy doesn't have to be the same as you and I,
Tommy doesn't need a reason if he wants to cry.
Tommy is a special soul and brings us so much joy,
Tommy is 1 of a kind he is my baby boy.

Taking Back Control- BPD

The Willow Tree
By Emma Warren

(A promise to my autistic son, who brings out the best parts of me, to provide a safe sanctuary in which he can grow and flourish in- post diagnosis)

To Finley, my promise to you.

At the bottom of the garden
There stands the willow tree,
If you look very closely
That is where you will find me.

In sight a rustic cottage so sweet,
Wood and stone surrounded by flowers complete.
Puffing smoke from the chimney above
Parceled with memories and love.

The sound of rustling grass and little footsteps draw near,
As you take my hand and say, "Mum I'm here".
I notice how calm and focused you've become because of our big open garden
You can now laugh and run.

As we go into the cottage
and sit at the table for tea.
You tell me about your day,
So happy, so free.

Going into the sitting room,
So comfortable, so kind.
I feel at ease,
At peace of mind.

My dear son, I love you just right.
Our life is blessed and good and now alright.
My dear son, I just want you to be okay,
One day I will take your barriers away.

Taking Back Control- BPD

I'm sorry to say that this place came from mummy's head,
But look very closely, look some years ahead...

In sight a rustic cottage so sweet.
At the bottom of the garden there stands the willow tree.
Take a look and you will see,
This is where we will be.

All my love Mum xxxx

Wednesday 13th November 2019
Finley aged 2 years and 11 months

Taking Back Control- BPD

Thank you to...

Sarah Eley- For everything!
Vicky Vaughan- Artist for BPD criteria
Borderline Arts Charity
A.C. Holloway- Author of 'Such is my fortune'
Jennifer. S. F. Raynor- Author of 'Such is my fortune'
Ashley Ferrari & Enchanted Fantasy Art- Community Art
Pippa Nayer- Community Art & their writing workshop
Carrie Raven- Community Art
Bethan Downs- Community Art Dance section
Jon Martin- Author of Healing crystals section
Adrienne Mason- Poem Author ASD section
Anne Ashcroft- Support & Editing
Martin Horsley- Book comedian!

Throughout the whole time of planning and writing this book, Martin has insisted on being in the book, and making me laugh on serval occasions when I thought publishing wasn't going to be possible. It's been a running joke for the past several months! So, congratulations Martin... you did make it into the book after all! <3

Taking Back Control- BPD

I would like to thank you once more for purchasing this book, supporting BPD, Borderline Arts and creating awareness for BPD. I am humbled by your active role in my vision of helping people to access support for their BPD, anxiety or other mental health issues.
I wish you well on your journey!

takingbackcontroleupd@gmail.com

Uniquely written with love
TAKING BACK CONTROL
We feel in colour.
We don't live with BPD...BPD lives with us!

What's next for Taking Back Control-BPD (Emma)?

My aim is to take Taking Back Control-BPD further than just a self-help book. Hopefully, transforming it into an ongoing community mental health project continuing to raise awareness for all mental health issues but especially BPD.

I want to emphasise that this isn't just about me, it's about bringing together a supportive community and letting others have their say too. Our society needs more people with mental health lived experience to speak out and help reduce the stigma associated with mental health issues.

My hope is that my Facebook page 'Taking Back Control-BPD' will become a platform for community kindness and support for those with BPD, ASD or generalised mental health issues. Everyone is welcome... diagnosis or not!

It's been a long-standing dream of mine to open and run a massive community project, sort of like a community hub, for people with mental health difficulties. Somewhere that is easily accessible to people struggling and supporting them for free or as affordably as possible. It has stemmed from my strong belief that no one should be rejected help and support.

This isn't just a book, it stands for way more than that, there is a bigger picture. There is obviously still a long way to go to make that picture a reality. The book and Facebook page are sort of a 'mini community hub' for creating awareness and ensuring that support is accessible to anyone struggling.

Join the support community at:

www.facebook.com/Taking.Back.Control.BPD

https://www.youtube.com/channel/UCxsukqEGeYAatFdcJHkyy9A

Printed in Great Britain
by Amazon